THE ULTIMATE GUIDE FOR BIPOLAR DISORDER

DEEPLY SUPPORTIVE AND HELPFUL RESOURCES FOR BIPOLAR I, BIPOLAR II, AND BIPOLAR RELATIONSHIPS

C.A. COOK

CONTENTS

Books and Audio books that bring hope into our world!

10% of the proceeds from this book are being donated
to iFred.org
to help continue their work with destigmatizing
depression and teaching Hope.

INTRODUCTION

Everyone in the world struggles with something. Family conflicts, financial issues, traumatic events—there is not a single person who hasn't experienced some kind of physical or emotional difficulty. For those who suffer from mental illnesses, experiencing such struggles can be a daily occurrence. Mental disorders and conditions, especially ones that go untreated, can make everyday tasks feel overwhelming–sometimes impossible. One mental illness, in particular, can feel like a neverending rollercoaster of chaos and frustration. This illness is known as bipolar disorder.

Bipolar disorder is a condition in which a person's mood fluctuates unpredictably, causing them to experience intense highs and lows. People all over the world have been diagnosed with the disorder and are fighting to find effective treatments. It is a serious condition that can be difficult to diagnose and can alter one's life immensely. Those with bipolar disorder may find it frightening to go through life, unsure of when their symptoms will strike; and it can feel extremely isolating due to the harmful stereotypes that currently exist regarding the disorder. Whether you are someone with bipolar disorder or have a loved one dealing with a diagnosis, the conflicting emotions and desperation for a solution can be exhausting. Rest assured, however, there is light at the end of the tunnel.

Doctors, scientists, and researchers alike have spent decades studying bipolar disorder and its effects on the mind and body. Every day, new discoveries open up doors to a better future for people affected by bipolar disorder. Treatments like medications, therapies, and lifestyle adjustments are becoming more and more popular among those diagnosed with the disorder, helping to improve lives and destigmatize what it means to be bipolar. Now more than ever, people with bipolar disorder are being given the chance to thrive.

In this book, you will be introduced to the truth about bipolar disorder. Through real-life stories and proven methodologies, *The Ultimate Guide for Bipolar Disorder* will teach you how to work with your or your loved one's diagnosis, instead of against it. You will learn the true definition of bipolar disorder, including its various subtypes, and what the process of receiving a diagnosis looks like. On top of that, we will compare common myths and misconceptions with scientific facts about the disorder, encouraging you to combat harmful stereotypes you may run into in your daily life.

In Chapter three, you will learn the importance of acknowledging when bipolar symptoms are damaging your life and relationships. When you can finally see past the fear of being judged or misunderstood, you enable yourself to seek the help you need. Treatment for this mental illness is crucial and the earlier you address the problems, the sooner you can begin your healing journey. Chapter three will delve into the many types of treatments one can receive for bipolar disorder, as well as certain lifestyle habits and tips that can greatly improve your daily life.

As you continue onto the next chapters, you will be encouraged to begin building your support system. Healing from the consequences of bipolar disorder does not have to be a lonely experience; establishing a solid group of mental health professionals, caring friends and family, and supportive peers can make a significant difference in your life. This team of people can lift you up when you feel overwhelmed by the responsibility of symptom management and provide you with the motivation you need to move forward with your treatment. The following chapters will show you how to reach out to others for help and build your team. You will learn communication techniques, feel inspired to educate your loved ones on bipolar disorder, and be given the tools to establish healthy boundaries.

From here, you will be introduced to "The Five Keys for Hope™," a method designed to increase hopefulness when all seems lost. No matter what you're going through during your treatment, having hope gives you the power to overcome it all. The methodology discussed in this book will teach you how to do just that. What's more, the final chapters will teach you specific techniques that have been proven to alleviate the stress of mental illness and create a more calming lifestyle. From routine creation to soulful meditation and affirmations, you will learn how to turn your bipolar disorder on its head and live a life that makes you happy.

Finally, at the end of our journey together, you will be provided with countless resources that can guide you further. Chapter eight is the place to find links to treatment and recovery centers, support groups, educational websites, and so much more—all dedicated to helping you conquer bipolar disorder and other mental illnesses. The end goal for this book is for you to feel fully equipped to master your healing and feel better than ever, regardless of your diagnosis. My hope is that the information and resources provided here will empower you to live a life that feels more centered and peaceful.

Want to start your day feeling centered and tapped into your heart-light?

Simply email me to receive a FREE 5-minute Meditation!

sunflowerhousepublishing@ yahoo.com

A NOTE FROM THE AUTHOR

During my lifetime—I'm in my 60s now—I have met many people who have struggled with various mental health diagnoses. Bipolar disorder, ADHD, borderline personality disorder, eating disorders, and codependency are just a few of the conditions I've observed. Almost everyone with whom I've spoken about this book has told me, "I had, or have, a relative or friend who struggles with bipolar disorder." Bipolar disorder impacts millions of people, including their friends, family, and colleagues. Mental health struggles affect more people than you may realize. I, personally, am recovering from my own struggles with codependency.

My self-development journey began when I was 30. During this time in my life, I was raising a one-year-old son while divorcing my husband, who was an alcoholic. My journey has taken me on many paths, including one-on-one psychotherapy, group experiential therapy, EMDR, and even alternative therapies like energy healing, reiki, meditation, and emotion code. I've also been part of an intensive leadership and self-development community for over 25 years now. I have learned and experienced that therapy, both traditional and alternative, as well as supportive journey companions, shaped the person I am today. Without it, I believe I would be trapped in a place of self-doubt, addictions, and suffering.

I want to be transparent by saying that I, myself, don't have bipolar disorder. However, I have friends who are diagnosed and hold deep compassion and empathy for anyone who suffers from the disorder. My experience has inspired me to widen my reach in an attempt to help people that have been touched by such a diagnosis. In this book, you will find an inspiring true story from a dear friend of mine who struggles with bipolar II disorder. His story is one of devastation and loss, as well as hope and triumph. It's included in this book as an example of how, even when you've hit rock bottom, there's a chance of rising again.

I am also excited to include a chapter on "The Five Keys for Hope," developed by my dear friend, Kathryn Goetzke. Kathryn has been spearheading major research on how hope is teachable, learnable, and measurable—something I've heard her say many times throughout our friendship. It's true, hope can be learned! In this book, you will be introduced to these five keys, as well as provided with links to resources where you can learn more about Kathryn's work and her company: Hopeful Mindsets. Another one of Kathryn's mantras is "it is always possible to get from hopelessness to hope if you have a roadmap." My sincere wish is that the tools in this book, including the Five Keys, will provide you with a roadmap for your journey of healing from the effects of bipolar disorder.

A little about me: I happen to be one of those people who *loves* organizing and compiling information. While exploring countless websites and articles about this disorder, I've experienced firsthand the frustration of trying to find comprehensive lists of valuable resources. To combat this frustration, in chapter eight I've tried my best to assemble as many resources as possible into one place, including finding providers, treatments, and support groups, as well as websites and apps offering research, tools and support for those struggling with bipolar disorder. I hope that this book will enable you to find the help you are seeking, without feeling lost or overwhelmed.

My thorough research on the subject and connections to folks with bipolar disorder have taught me that treatment is possible, no matter who you are. The following chapters are here to show you how to live a life in which suffering is not a daily occurrence, but joy and pleasure are. While I encourage you to read each chapter, this book is written so that you may go directly to chapter eight to find all the pertinent resources you need, or to chapter four to gain some inner peace from the meditations that are provided. You do not have to read the chapters in chronological order to learn from them. Take a look at the table of contents and see which chapters call to you.

The most important step in helping those with mental illness is to teach the world that having a disorder is absolutely nothing of which to be ashamed or scared. There IS hope!

–C.A. Cook

1

A TRUE STORY OF HOPE
Told by Don

Let me (Don) start with a bit of background about my life because all of this is what my doctor and I eventually concluded led to my bipolar episode. I also want to forewarn you that some of my story is graphic in nature. But it was part of my authentic story, so I didn't want to leave it out. I just wanted you to know in advance that some parts may be harder than others to read.

My first wife and I were married when we were in our 20s. I worked for a large bank and made a good salary. We moved a few times for my job and had two children – a boy and a girl. Sadly, when my wife was in her late-30s she was diagnosed with cancer and died from it within eight months. That was a VERY hard thing to go through. Our children were 10 and 13 and I was suddenly a single dad with 2 kids. It was a lot. But I did the best I could raising them, taking them to dance lessons and soccer and all the things kids do, while working for the bank in a very stressful job

I met my second wife several years later. My kids loved her, and I was so grateful for that. She also had a son from a previous marriage, so we became a blended family.

I continued getting promotions at the bank, ending up as a senior vice president making a six-figure income. I was doing really well!

After 25 years at the bank, I left to become a motivational speaker and author, which was something I felt called to do. I ended up creating a multi-week course and was able to sell it to corporations for their staff, and that led to more and more speaking opportunities. I really felt like I was in my element. I ended up speaking in 12 countries, writing books, and making a lot of money.

With my second wife, I thought that I had reached Nirvana with the person I married. Honestly, we did everything together. Our friends would say "you are like two peas in a pod." We owned a condominium at the beach, and both loved going there. We had the same kind of sense of humor AND she was drop-dead gorgeous. I told her all the time how beautiful she was! I was actually in awe of my good luck of having met her. I was totally in love. We had all the comforts of a big house, nice cars, doing fun recreational things like golfing and tennis...it looked pretty perfect from the outside.

We were working in the business together – she was handling the bookings and the business side of things. Things started shifting in the marriage when I noticed that she had started drinking. Because I'd never been around alcoholism - and because she had never displayed any characteristics of an alcoholic, I didn't see it coming...except that we would get home from work, and then not too long after that she would pass out. The tipping point was one weekend when she went to visit her sister. I wanted to go to the pool, so I was trying to find the suntan lotion and, after searching everywhere, I looked in the guest bedroom closet. There were at least 20 bottles of vodka, in various states of consumption and flavors, on the closet floor. The first thing that struck me was why is this here? We had a wet bar – and were empty nesters by that time, so why would there be vodka in this closet? I just waited until she got home to talk with her about it. She was in a great mood until I told her about what I found. She immediately became hostile to me. I can't emphasize enough how much I loved her, so I thought we could get her help. But she said she didn't need help.

This went on for several more months. She'd get drunk when we came home and pass out. And, of course, this caused other issues. I was still totally in love with this woman and willing to do anything, so I suggested we go to counseling. She agreed, but she would show up drunk at the sessions about half the time. And then in the counseling session, she started accusing me of cheating on her. I didn't - I'm not that kind of person. I wouldn't have thought for a second about taking a chance on screwing up my relationship with her by doing that! The counselor asked her if she had some kind of evidence, and she would just say "a woman knows." I can't tell you how many tears I shed in those sessions. Feeling like she was just slipping through my fingers. I would have gone to war or protected her from anything to have kept my relationship with her.

It was our counselor that finally suggested we separate and get a divorce. She said, "I don't tell many people that I'm doing marriage counseling with to just stop and quit, but I just don't see you two being compatible anymore." I was devastated.

I moved to an apartment within a five-minute drive of where the house was. For at least a month she called me every night and begged me to come over and spend the night with her because she was scared. I'd go over there because I didn't want to be mean. But my heart was broken – it was SO broken.

Well, eventually, I realized that for the first time in my life, I had money AND I didn't have anybody to support, including children. I'm a nice-looking guy and was in good shape so I started joining dating apps and was going out five or six nights a week on dates with different women. I'd take them on exotic trips, and we'd go to expensive restaurants. On several occasions, I'd buy a round of drinks for everyone in the bar! I bought a boat…and one week I bought five cars.

This was so far out of my character, it seemed ridiculous. But at the time it felt perfectly normal for a guy who's got money and who loves people. At least that's how I justified it to myself. I mean, I'm somebody who cares about people and we're having fun, and why not?

Somehow, in my manic state (which I didn't realize I was in) I didn't think I needed to work. I was just having a good time. I went through millions of dollars.

When I finally realized that I was running out of money I started calling my friends who DID have money and asking them for large loans. They trusted me and gave me the money. I never paid them back. I got a big loan from my mom. I couldn't pay it back. I was still trying to live this large lifestyle on borrowed money. It wasn't until the walls started crumbling that my relationship with everyone changed.

I'd say this manic phase lasted a year or so. Then it turned to depression. I started hearing what I thought was God telling me to go help people.

Remember, I didn't have much money at this point. I had a car, but it was VERY low on gas. I have a vivid memory of one time when God told me to get in the car and drive. I was following where God was telling me to go, and I ended up in the middle of nowhere. Then I heard God say "Don, you see that light over in the distance? I haven't been really honest with you, Don. There are some people from another planet down here. And they're a little timid about how to make their entry into planet Earth." By now it was 3 or 4 a.m. It's in the middle of winter and I have no gas. So, I'm trying to communicate back to God. "God, I have no gas." "You're driving on God's gas, Don…you're driving on God's gas," he said. I'm not sure how I got home but somehow, I did.

Nobody knew my thoughts. Nobody knew what I was going through. I felt like I was crazy.

I reached out to the therapist whom we had seen for marriage counseling but for some reason (maybe because it was so NOT me) she didn't think I was manic, but, through a doctor she worked with, was able to prescribe some meds for me. In hindsight, that was a really bad decision.

My ex-wife and I still shared a dog and occasionally she would bring him over for me to keep him. I really loved that dog. This particular time though, I felt like everything was crashing around me. I had let SO many people down. I decided I was going to commit suicide. I wrote a suicide note and took the whole bottle of meds. My ex came to pick up the dog, finding me passed out, along with the note. She, of course, called 911. They took me to the psychiatric hospital where I stayed for several weeks. I hated being there, but I soon realized that to get out I had to play along with the doctor. All the while, I was still thinking "once I get out of here, I can REALLY commit suicide and be done with this life I messed up so much."

My ex came to pick me up and helped me to get a cheap car, and let me stay at her house for a few days until I had to leave. Her son was coming into town and by this time he knew what was going on with me and didn't want me anywhere near his mom.

I got in the car and started driving very fast on the interstate. At 75+ miles an hour, I purposefully veered the car off the road and down an embankment. The car flipped five times and I landed standing up inside the car with it upside down. I was totally unscathed. I only had a couple of scratches. That was it. "Oh my god! Why can't I die?!" is what was going through my head.

The police came and said I didn't need to go to the hospital. But I didn't know what to do, so I called my ex-wife and asked if she would come to get me.

She came and took me back to her house, but her son was there, and he was very angry with me because he was convinced that I was the reason his mom started drinking. He was yelling at me to leave…but I literally had nowhere to go. He called the police. My ex was so distraught over all of this, but she also didn't want to lose her son. The police came and took me away.

They ended up dropping me off at a convenience store, telling me NOT to go back to that house or they would arrest me again. I had a little bit of money so I went inside and bought a glass bottle of something to drink. There were some woods across the street so I just walked in the woods and found something hard that I could use to break the glass bottle with. I started cutting my throat and wrists and legs. And here's the thing that I remember more than anything else... I didn't feel it. I was in so much emotional pain that the physical pain did not hurt. I didn't scream, I didn't even make a sound.

These two or three teenagers just happened to be walking in the woods and walked up on me. It scared them to death. They called 911. When the medics got there, I remember one of them saying they didn't think they were going to be able to save this one. I mean, I was close. And I remember thinking, thank God, this is going to be over. I thought, okay, this is finally what needs to happen.

I woke up the next morning with bandages all over my throat, my wrists, and my legs, and strapped down to a bed. There was a nurse in the room – I could tell I was on suicide watch. I realized I was still alive and that made me SO pissed off that I started screaming and yelling as loud as I could over and over. They quickly gave me a shot to calm me down.

Later that day I found out that my son had called me. When we were able to talk he was beside himself – I'd never heard his voice in that much agony. He said "Dad, please stop this, please, I will do whatever I have to do. You name it, I will do whatever! I need my dad." The pain I heard in him was a turning point for me. I asked him if he could call me every day. And he said, "absolutely." And I said, "I'm willing to hang in there for as long as I have to you if you just call me every day." So, for the next few months, he called me every day.

After a few days, they admitted me to the psychiatric hospital and I started seeing a really good psychiatrist. He got me on the right meds, and I met with him a couple of times a week. There were also support group meetings I attended. He also could tell that I wasn't a "street smart" kind of guy so he made arrangements for me to be in the program until the social worker could get my social security started (I was 62 then and was eligible to get it) and then was able to help me get into an apartment where I'd be safe. I was in the inpatient program for about 6 weeks and then after that, I was in the outpatient program.

He diagnosed me with bipolar disorder and explained that it was triggered by the two catastrophic events that happened – my wife getting cancer and dying, and then the trauma of the divorce from a woman I loved SO much. He also believed that it was genetic. I was so thankful for this doctor because finally, someone had helped me make some sense of what was happening to me.

I ended up seeing him years later and I asked him if he'd like to get a cup of coffee. We did and I told him that he saved my life.

That all happened many years ago – I'm in my mid-70s now – and I am SO grateful to be alive! I kept taking my meds and attending the outpatient program which helped me to get back on my feet. I picked up my guitar again and started playing and writing songs. Songs that had A LOT of meaning to them. I found a church that had a music team and they invited me to join in. I started making new friends. My faith in a Higher Power grew stronger. I even found a singing partner whose voice fit perfectly with mine when we would sing together. She loved my songs, and we started singing them together and even recorded two CDs of my original songs! Songs that would never have been written if I had been successful so many years ago in taking my own life. (I've included one at the end of this story.) I'm by no means in the financial bracket I used to be in, but I have a nice apartment, food, clothing, and all my needs are met.

I've shared my story so that you will know that even in your darkest days you are worthy of living! What helped me the most was going to a facility that could help me. Finding a doctor that cared. Being treated with medication and therapy and group support. Having a loving family member who never gave up on me. And having a deep faith in a Higher Power whom I choose to call God.

I sincerely hope that you don't have to go through the dark times like I did before you ask for help. There is so much support available to you. Reach out. It's OK. You are worth it!

SOMEBODY LOVES YOU © 2015

(Recording on audiobook performed by Cindy Ballaro and Paul Huff with musical arrangement by Fred Story)

VERSE I
WHEN THE RAINY STORMS OF LIFE
   ARE RAGING HIGH
WHEN THE TEMPEST BREAKS AND
   TEARS OPEN YOUR SKY
WHEN THE TEARS JUST WON'T STOP
   AND YOUR PLANS ARE IN THE DUST
WHEN YOUR SOUL HAS BEEN ROBBED
   & YOUR HOPES HAVE BEEN
   CRUSHED

CHORUS I
IN CLOUDS OR SUNSHINE, IN
   DARKNESS, AND BRIGHT
IN EVENING SHADOWS AND IN
   MORNING LIGHT

SOMEBODY LOVES YOU, KNOWS YOU
*   BY NAME*
KNOWS WHEN YOU'RE LOST, LOVES
*   YOU JUST THE SAME*
SOMEBODY HEARD YOU BEFORE YOU
*   UTTERED A SOUND*
LEFT A HARVEST FOR YOU AT BIRTH
*   THAT COVERED THE GROUND*
OH, SOMEBODY, SOMEBODY
*   LOVES YOU*

VERSE II

WHEN SORROW FILLS YOUR HEART AS
*   YOU TROD ALONG YOUR WAY*
AND YOU QUESTION YOUR FAITH
*   WITH FRESH TRIALS EACH DAY*
WHEN THE NEWS THAT YOU GET IS
*   MORE THAN YOU CAN BEAR*
KNOW THAT SOMEBODY LOVES YOU,
*   AND IS PRESENT RIGHT THERE*

CHORUS I

IN CLOUDS OR SUNSHINE, IN
*   DARKNESS, AND BRIGHT*
IN EVENING SHADOWS AND IN
*   MORNING LIGHT*

SOMEBODY LOVES YOU, KNOWS YOU
    BY NAME
KNOWS WHEN YOU'RE LOST, LOVES
    YOU JUST THE SAME
SOMEBODY HEARD YOU BEFORE YOU
    UTTERED A SOUND
LEFT A HARVEST FOR YOU AT BIRTH
    THAT COVERED THE GROUND
OH, SOMEBODY, SOMEBODY
    LOVES YOU

CHORUS II
SOMEBODY LOVES YOU AND LONGS
    FOR YOUR WILL
TO FOLLOW THEM HOME, THEIR WISH
    TO FULFILL
THEY ARE RICH AND HAVE MANSIONS
    AND FIELDS THAT ARE WIDE
WANTS TO FILL YOU WHEN YOU FEEL
    EMPTY INSIDE

TAG
OH, SOMEBODY, SOMEBODY
    LOVES YOU
OH SOMEBODY, OH SOMEBODY, GOD
    LOVES YOU

2

THE MANY FACES OF BIPOLAR

When you think of bipolar disorder, what comes to mind? Perhaps you have just been diagnosed, after what feels like a lifetime of inner turmoil and confusion. Maybe you received a diagnosis so long ago that you've lost sight of where your bipolar symptoms end and your true self begins. Or maybe you are desperately looking for a diagnosis that fits your symptoms, and you've heard that bipolar disorder may be it. You may even have a loved one with bipolar disorder and are trying to learn more about their experience and how you can help them. Whatever the case may be, it's important that you understand the ins and outs of the illness and how it can be treated, so that you can move forward in a more positive, fulfilling direction.

This chapter will serve as your in-depth introduction to bipolar disorder, from the different types of bipolar to the many ways you can manage your symptoms and everything in between. Once you have a solid grasp on the disorder, you will be able to better understand how to adjust your life to your diagnosis, without feeling like you have to sacrifice what you love.

WHAT IS BIPOLAR DISORDER?

Today, nearly three percent of Americans have been diagnosed with bipolar disorder. You may be thinking, *three percent isn't that much, that means 97 percent of people aren't bipolar.* While you're not wrong, but three percent of the United States population is roughly 10,029,000 people. Over ten million people in America are dealing with daily occurrences of intense mood swings, racing thoughts, depressive episodes, and so much more—all at once. *Ten million people.* That means there are more people in the United States living with bipolar disorder than there are people living in Alabama, Montana, and Nevada *combined* (World Population Review, 2020). In order for all of these people to receive the help they need, the types, causes, and treatments for bipolar disorder need to be discussed.

Simply put, bipolar disorder is a neurological brain disorder that causes unusual mood changes, energy shifts, and difficulty completing ordinary tasks as expected. People with the disorder often experience episodes of mania and depression, meaning they feel extreme emotional highs and lows. A manic episode is an emotional circumstance that causes someone to feel unusually energetic and euphoric. Mania can also cause feelings of agitation, anxiety, and nervousness. Sometimes, these feelings are felt all at once. Other times, just a few of them occur. Other symptoms of mania are common in people diagnosed with bipolar disorder, such as high distractibility and a decreased need for sleep. On the other side of the coin, a depressive episode is described by a notable loss of interest or pleasure in activities, significant fluctuations in weight, sleep difficulties, and an overall feeling of worthlessness and hopelessness. Depression can also lead to more dangerous circumstances, including uncontrollable fatigue and suicidal ideation or intention.

On top of that, those with a bipolar diagnosis may experience comorbidities, meaning illnesses or conditions that occur alongside their bipolar disorder. Common comorbidities include eating disorders, ADHD, and substance use disorders. Being diagnosed as bipolar can be overwhelming and disappointing, but it can be treated.

Types of Bipolar Disorder

There are three distinct types of bipolar disorder, in addition to unspecified or comorbid bipolar disorder. Each type has its own specific symptoms and treatments, making it absolutely crucial for people to be diagnosed as accurately as possible.

Bipolar I

Bipolar I is most commonly diagnosed in people who have experienced at least one manic episode, typically followed or preceded by a less intense sense of mania (hypomania) or a depressive episode. Manic episodes contributed to bipolar I typically last at least seven days, for most or all of the day, or are so severe that they require hospitalization right away. Depressive episodes contributed to bipolar I can last for up to two weeks. A mixture of manic and depressive episodes throughout a long period of time is also possible with this type of bipolar disorder.

Bipolar II

Similarly to bipolar I, bipolar II includes the experience of at least one major depressive episode and one hypomanic episode. Hypomania is a less severe type of mania, but still involves many of the same symptoms on a smaller scale. According to the Mayo Clinic

(2021a), to be diagnosed with bipolar II, a person will have experienced a depressive or hypomanic episode in their lifetime, but not a full-scale manic episode.

Cyclothymic Disorder

This version of bipolar disorder, also called cyclothymia, is less severe than both bipolar I and II. It involves many of the symptoms shown with mania and depression, though they are not frequent or intense enough to be considered a manic/depressive episode. Cyclothymia is "a chronically unstable mood state in which people experience hypomania and mild depression for at least two years" (NAMI, 2020).

Unspecified or Other Specified Bipolar

Sometimes, a person shows symptoms of bipolar disorder that are inconsistent with one specific type of the illness. In this case, they would most likely be diagnosed with "unspecified" bipolar disorder. Oftentimes, the person experiences abnormal mood shifts that resemble those of someone with bipolar I, II, or cyclothymia. However, their doctor or mental health professional cannot contribute their mood changes to one distinct type.

It is not uncommon for someone with unspecified bipolar disorder to be experiencing conflicting symptoms, such as those from another mental illness or medical issue. For example, someone with symptoms of bipolar disorder may have other symptoms that are induced by drugs and alcohol. It's also possible that conditions like multiple sclerosis or stroke can conflict with a person's bipolar disorder diagnosis, leaving them unspecified.

CAUSES OF BIPOLAR DISORDER

If you have been diagnosed with bipolar disorder, you must know one thing: your mental illness is not your fault! No matter how hard your brain, or someone in your life, tries to convince you that you did something to cause your bipolar disorder, remind yourself of the truth. Bipolar disorder infiltrates the brain, causing countless physical and emotional symptoms that are out of your biological control.

If you have a loved one with bipolar disorder, remind them that their diagnosis is out of their control, but their treatment is not. It can be quite disheartening to receive such a life-changing diagnosis, especially when you feel as though nobody in your life will understand. Being the family or close friend of someone with the disorder allows you to aid them in their treatment, act as their confidant, and be an active member of their support system. Instead of reinforcing harmful stigma, let them know that the behaviors stemming from their bipolar disorder are not their fault. Hearing this may be exactly what your loved one needs to release any feelings of guilt or shame surrounding their diagnosis.

It has been scientifically proven that the disorder is caused by various factors; genetics, internal and external triggers, and chemical imbalances in the brain are just a few. There is not one specific issue that can be attributed to your diagnosis, at least not one that has been discovered over the past several decades of research.

Genetic Causes

As it stands, no single gene has been shown to cause bipolar disorder. Rather, a person's genetic makeup is what can increase their chances of developing the disorder. Experts have found that a person with a family history of bipolar disorder is statistically more likely to develop the disorder themselves (NAMI, 2020). The risk is higher, but it is not guaranteed.

Neurological Causes

Researchers theorize that a person's brain structure and functional ability may also cause bipolar disorder. Although x-rays and brain scans cannot be used alone to accurately diagnose someone, studies have proven that people with bipolar disorder have noticeable differences in their brain's anatomy compared to those without the disorder (NIMH, 2020). In addition, chemical imbalances are shown to contribute to a person's development of mental illnesses, including bipolar disorder. Neurotransmitters that influence emotions and adrenaline, namely serotonin and dopamine, possibly induce the emotional symptoms of mania, hypomania, and depression.

Symptom Triggers

The symptoms of bipolar disorder are frequently impacted by forces outside of the brain and DNA structure, too. Physical environments, injuries and illnesses, relationship conflicts, and more are all potential stressors for manic and depressive episodes. Imagine you are having an ordinary day, one without any noticeable problems or complications. Suddenly, you get a notification on your phone that something terrible has happened. A death in the family, a diagnosis of a serious illness, or a break-up are all stressful events, what many would call "triggers."

These triggers, along with many others, can cause someone's symptoms of bipolar disorder to surge, resulting in the onset of mania or depression. In some cases, a person experiencing such triggers may not yet know that they have bipolar disorder, leading them to question why they are having such an intense emotional and physical reaction. On a more positive note, this may encourage the person to seek help and get diagnosed, leading to the management of their symptoms and triggers.

Sleep disturbances and difficulties, histories of abuse, and financial problems are also common triggers for anyone struggling with their mental health.

REACHING A DIAGNOSIS

Because the symptoms of every type of bipolar disorder are so similar to each other, as well as to other mental health conditions like major depressive disorder, it can be incredibly difficult to get an accurate diagnosis. For many people struggling with bipolar symptoms, it can help for a close family member or friend to recognize when the person seems off. Acknowledging when their loved one is more withdrawn than usual without apparent cause, for example, may encourage them to seek help.

On the contrary, someone who is good at hiding their depressive symptoms and presents as a relatively pleasant person may not be perceived as a candidate for a bipolar diagnosis. Sometimes, it takes extreme behaviors and mood changes for a person's support system to notice when something deeper is going on. Nonetheless, whether the symptoms of bipolar disorder are obvious or discrete, getting diagnosed is the most important step in receiving treatment. Without proper help, your bipolar disorder may worsen over time.

The most important part of reaching an accurate diagnosis is identifying your symptoms early and being completely honest with your doctor about what you are experiencing. It may be helpful to keep a written list of the symptoms you have been experiencing, as well as any questions you have or behavioral concerns you've had recently. For many people, being prepared for an important doctor appointment is the key to receiving the help they need.

It can be extremely uncomfortable to discuss certain topics, especially with someone who is not a close friend or family member, but it will benefit you in the long run. Your health is a top priority and should be treated as such. Remember, your doctor should be a person you trust and feel safe speaking to. Do not be afraid to ask what experience your doctor has with bipolar disorder and other mental illnesses. If they are a general practitioner, their experience may be limited, but they should have plenty of resources and advice to guide you in getting the treatment that will work best for you.

Common Behaviors Shown During Depressive Episodes

The following list will highlight some of the most common behaviors exhibited by someone experiencing a **depressive episode** as a result of their bipolar disorder:

- Feeling withdrawn, sad, hopeless, worthless, or numb to emotion
- Crying and expressing melancholy more than usual
- Losing interest in activities that were once enjoyable
- Feeling no pleasure from favored hobbies and tasks
- Losing weight without trying or gaining weight rapidly
- Feeling uninterested in or unable to eat
- Sleeping too much or not enough
- Having difficulty falling asleep or staying asleep
- Feeling restless or moving slower than usual

- Experiencing fatigue and a significant loss of energy
- Feeling excessive guilt or shame without adequate reasoning
- Having difficulty concentrating or sticking to one thought
- Being unable to make a decision
- Thinking about and/or planning death or attempting suicide

Common Behaviors Shown During Manic Episodes

The following list will highlight some of the most common behaviors exhibited by someone experiencing a **manic episode** as a result of their bipolar disorder:

- Acting more jittery, jumpy, or tense than usual
- Feeling more energized or exhibiting an increase in activity
- Feeling intense euphoria or an inflated sense of well-being (grandiosity)
- Sleeping much less than usual

- Talking excessively or more animatedly than usual
- Experiencing uncontrollable thoughts and rumination
- Being easily distracted and frequently moving from one activity to another
- Limited impulse control and inability to make responsible decisions
- Feeling indestructible or able to do anything

Diagnosing bipolar disorder, regardless of the type, requires intensive testing by a qualified doctor or mental health professional. Physical exams, mood and behavior questionnaires, and private discussions are all necessary components of achieving an accurate diagnosis. It is so much more than talking to your doctor and getting an answer right off the bat. In addition to mental health-focused testing, your doctor may test you for multiple conditions in order to rule out other possibilities. Blood tests and brain scans may be ordered in this case.

If other conditions or mental illnesses have been ruled out, your behaviors and symptoms will be compared to the guidelines for diagnosing bipolar disorder. The Diagnostic and Statistical Manual of Mental Disorders (DSM) is used by most, if not all, healthcare professionals to make diagnoses. The DSM is a thorough collection of guidelines and diagnostic information for mental illnesses. Your doctor or mental health professional will likely use these guidelines to determine which type of bipolar disorder best fits the symptoms you are experiencing.

Try not to go into your first appointment with your doctor with the expectation that you will leave with a firm diagnosis. It can take multiple appointments or psychiatric sessions to reach a decision about your symptoms. Your doctor or psychiatrist may ask you to keep track of your moods and behaviors for a certain amount of days in order for them to have a good understanding of your current emotional state. It is also possible that, with your consent, they will ask your loved ones about your symptoms and behaviors. This typically happens for younger people, such as older children and teens.

To be diagnosed with any type of bipolar disorder, a person must have experienced at least one episode of mania or hypomania. Depending on the situation, there may also be other symptom requirements, such as having at least three or more symptoms simultaneously before, during, or after an episode. Most diagnoses happen during the older teen or adult years, however, there are children who have been diagnosed, as well (NIMH, 2020).

You may be unsure about whether or not the behaviors you have been exhibiting are, in fact, symptoms of bipolar disorder. In this case, take a moment to reflect on the past few weeks or months. Have you felt as though you need less sleep than usual? Are you restless or easily agitated, likely without knowing why? Do you sometimes feel overconfident, or act on strong urges without thinking of the consequences? Do you often feel jumpy, jittery, or quick to get angry? How often do you go through phases of feeling withdrawn or sad for no apparent reason? These are all behaviors commonly shown by people with bipolar disorder. Even if you are hesitant about bringing it up to a doctor, know that it is always better to be safe than sorry. If your behaviors are powerful enough to make you question your mental well-being, they are powerful enough to be evaluated by a professional.

Keep in mind, the earlier you address your bipolar symptoms, the earlier you can begin to manage them. The healthcare system in the United States can be particularly discouraging and it can sometimes take a long time to find the support you need. Having patience and staying resilient in the face of healthcare challenges are the keys to receiving sufficient treatment.

There are countless websites, support groups, and foundations that are dedicated to guiding people through the complexities of bipolar disorder. At the end of this book, you will be provided with a comprehensive list of resources designed to help you find the support you need.

PROVING STEREOTYPES WRONG

Mental illnesses affect so many people and, thankfully, are becoming less stigmatized every day. Unfortunately, however, there are still plenty of harmful stereotypes and common misconceptions that exist about bipolar disorder. With such negativity and misunderstanding about the disorder, many people may hide their true experiences and neglect their own health out of fear of being judged or discriminated against. No one wants to be the person with "problems," nor do they want to deal with the questions that come with being open about your illness.

In books and movies, it's not uncommon to see characters diagnosed with bipolar disorder being portrayed as "crazy" or uncontrollable. The media also plays a powerful role in spreading misinformation about the disorder. In the past few years, the term *bipolar* has become a popular adjective, instead of its true meaning. It is sometimes used to describe an unpredictable or troublesome situation: "My mom was being bipolar today about letting me hang out at the mall" or "my phone is so bipolar, it keeps shutting off and turning back on for no reason" are examples of how the term has been used. Not only are these uses of the term "bipolar" incorrect, but they contribute to a widespread misconception that being bipolar is a personality trait, rather than an illness with serious consequences.

The only way to combat such stereotypes is to educate yourself on the truth and advocate for it. Once you have the knowledge, you can use it to show other people what it is really like to live with a bipolar diagnosis.

Many people contribute to the perpetuation of negative stereotypes, often without even realizing it. You may be someone who has a close relationship with your family, keeping them up to date with your health whenever you can. Maybe you've overheard your parents telling someone about your bipolar disorder and accidentally saying something that isn't accurate. While they are trying their best to be sympathetic to your situation, you can't help but feel frustrated that they don't fully understand. Even doctors can spread misinformation about the disorder if they have not had enough experience diagnosing or recognizing it. This is where your knowledge about your mental experience is an asset.

You can use it to change how the world views people with bipolar diagnoses, even if it just starts in your inner circle.

Myths, Misconceptions, and the Truth About Bipolar Disorder

The list below discusses common myths and misconceptions people have about bipolar disorder:

Myth: Having bipolar disorder just means you have a lot of mood swings.

- **Fact:** Bipolar disorder is much more than simple mood swings. Someone with a bipolar diagnosis typically experiences intense moods that last several days, sometimes even weeks. Generally, the person will not switch from depressed to manic in a matter of hours, nor will they go from one feeling to another multiple times a day.

Myth: All people with bipolar disorder act the same.

- **Fact:** Everybody is a unique individual, regardless of their mental diagnosis. People with bipolar disorder experience a variety of symptoms that differ depending on their personal situations, treatment plan, and more.

Myth: Your kid can't have bipolar disorder. They're probably just naughty or seeking attention.

- **Fact:** Children can absolutely be diagnosed with bipolar disorder. While it may be more challenging to diagnose, young kids and teens are not immune to developing the disorder. Often, however, kids are diagnosed with behavioral conditions or ADHD (Attention Deficit/Hyperactivity Disorder) before they are diagnosed with a mood disorder.

Myth: Bipolar people are too unstable to have a steady job or lifestyle.

- **Fact:** Having a stable life while dealing with bipolar disorder is far from impossible. In fact, it is not so different from working and dealing with any other emotional or mental illness. Having a steady job or stable lifestyle along with bipolar disorder is entirely possible, it just requires consistent symptom management and self-awareness.

Myth: You're not bipolar, you're just moody and using a disorder as an excuse for your bad behavior.

- **Fact:** People with bipolar disorder have little to no control over their changes in mood, and are less able to control their behavior when their moods fluctuate to extreme levels. Bipolar disorder affects the brain and is proven through several tests—it is not an excuse.

Myth: Being manic must make you so happy and productive.

- **Fact:** Mania and manic episodes can cause a person to feel energized enough to perform necessary tasks. However, it can be difficult to control and can result in being out of touch with reality. This may do more harm than good, as it can cause a person to make reckless decisions and harm themselves or the people around them.

Myth: You can fix your bipolar disorder by exercising and eating better.

- **Fact:** Despite the decades of research and advocacy done for bipolar disorder, a cure has not yet been found. However, with individualized treatment and consistent lifestyle adjustments, people with bipolar disorder can live fulfilling and happy lives.

Myth: Bipolar medications will eliminate a person's creativity and passion for life.

- **Fact:** It's easy to believe that certain treatments can and will make someone lose their "creative spark," but that's not actually the case. For some people, going on medication or seeing a therapist can help them think more clearly and focus on their creative endeavors.

Myth: Misusing drugs and alcohol will cause someone to become bipolar.

- **Fact:** Substance use has never been proven to cause bipolar disorder. There are times when someone's use of drugs or alcohol can exacerbate their existing symptoms, but it cannot cause bipolar disorder in anyone. It's important to note that misusing substances while diagnosed with bipolar disorder, and receiving medical treatment, can severely impact your health and well-being.

Myth: Bipolar disorder is very rare.

- **Fact:** Though three percent of the US population seems like a small amount, it means that millions of people across the country are dealing with very intense and troubling emotions. Bipolar disorder may not be as common as other conditions, like anxiety or depression, but it affects more people than one might think. The statistics regarding the number of people currently diagnosed with the disorder are also limited to those who seek professional help. Because of stereotypes and misconceptions, which often lead to misdiagnosis, many people may have bipolar disorder but have not received a proper diagnosis or treatment.

Now that you are aware of the facts and common myths surrounding the disorder, use your knowledge to educate others! Whether you have bipolar disorder, or know someone who does, you can play a crucial role in raising worldwide awareness and acceptance.

BIPOLAR DISORDER QUIZ

If you believe you show the signs and symptoms of bipolar disorder, know that there are plenty of ways to get help. The quiz linked below can give you a better understanding of the frequency of your symptoms and help you decide if you should speak with your doctor about getting tested for bipolar disorder. To receive the most accurate quiz results, answer each question in regard to how you usually feel or act.

www.psychcentral.com/quizzes/bipolar-quiz

The results of this quiz should be used as a helpful guide, not a professional medical diagnosis. If you are experiencing symptoms that raise concern or inhibit your ability to live your daily life, speak to your doctor about getting evaluated for bipolar disorder.

Being affected by bipolar disorder, either through your own or a loved one's diagnosis, can feel overwhelming and isolating—but it can and will get better. There are several treatments, lifestyle changes, and support groups that can ease the frustrations of bipolar symptoms and behaviors.

Disclaimer: *This quiz is not a diagnostic tool and will not give you an accurate diagnosis of bipolar disorder. It simply serves as a guide for tracking and understanding any symptoms you are experiencing.*

Key Takeaway:

Bipolar disorder is a complex, life-changing mental illness that affects a person's ability to regulate emotions and energy levels. The condition is made up of various subtypes and symptoms, ranging from persistent depression to episodes of total euphoria. There are many causes of bipolar disorder that include genetic and neurological factors, as well as countless harmful stereotypes that exist about people with a bipolar diagnosis. Although it is currently incurable, a life with the condition does not have to be as scary or overwhelming as you may think.

3

STARTING TO HEAL

Before you can get treated for your bipolar disorder, you must be capable of asking for support. Admitting that something is wrong, especially in regard to mental health, requires a certain amount of vulnerability. The only way anyone can help you is if you are willing to help yourself. To reach this level of vulnerability, it's imperative that you can understand and acknowledge the negative impact your symptoms have on your life and relationships with people you care about. Additionally, you cannot let the stigma of having bipolar disorder prevent you from reaching out to your support system or healthcare professionals.

Acknowledging the true nature of your symptoms can open you up to a world of possibility. By accepting that you may have a mental illness, you take control of your symptoms. Rather than letting your symptoms determine how you live your life, you give yourself the power to decide how to move forward. Acknowledgment leads to self-empowerment, which in turn leads to successful treatment.

Treating your bipolar symptoms and behaviors can change your life in more ways than you can imagine. While treatment is great for lessening the physical and emotional toll bipolar disorder takes on you, it can also alleviate any tension you have in your relationships. Suffering from untreated symptoms will likely cause you to experience conflicts with the people you care most about. All too often, people with untreated bipolar disorder have difficulty maintaining communication and healthy boundaries. After you learn how to manage those symptoms, you can take the necessary steps toward healing any damaged relationships, whether they are romantic or with colleagues, friends, and family.

FINDING THE RIGHT TREATMENT

Typical treatments for bipolar disorder work to decrease the severity and frequency of manic, hypomanic, and depressive episodes. Though the disorder cannot currently be cured, lessening the daily struggles helps people live more comfortably. Leaving your bipolar symptoms untreated can also result in dangerous consequences. Choosing to not receive any treatment may feel like the option that requires less self-work, but it will most likely damage your overall well-being, along with the aspects of your daily life that bring you joy and fulfillment.

The National Health Service (NHS) in the United Kingdom reports that untreated bipolar disorder may lead to longer episodes of mania and depression. According to their website, going untreated can lengthen episodes of mania to at least three months, sometimes as long as six. Depressive episodes can last even longer, from six months to an entire year (NHS, 2021b). With treatment that is individualized and effective, the length of such episodes can decrease significantly.

In an article published by the American Journal of Psychiatry, researchers concluded that bipolar disorder progresses over time, leading to damage to a person's hippocampus (Mojica Rey, 2003). The hippocampus is a region of the human brain that is responsible for regulating emotions and memory. When this area is damaged or dysfunctional, the brain has more difficulty retaining new memories, balancing emotions, and producing new neurons—functions that make treatments like therapy and emotional growth possible.

Treating bipolar disorder as early as possible will help slow down the damage the illness does to the brain. In the research study mentioned above, medications are discussed as a potential way of regaining brain function and the ability to reverse the damage done by the disorder.

Finally, leaving your bipolar disorder untreated may make a person act on risky impulses. On the less harmful side, a bipolar person might spend their money carelessly, ruining their financial stability. In the same vein, someone acting on impulse could quit their job without forethought or hurt relationships that truly mean something to them. On a more perilous note, untreated bipolar disorder can cause someone to drive recklessly, engage in dangerous activities, abuse substances, or even attempt suicide. In fact, research has shown that suicide rates for people with bipolar disorder are 10 to 30 times higher than the general population. Additionally, up to 20% of "mostly untreated" people with bipolar disorder die by suicide (Dome et al., 2019). These numbers are alarming and show just how important it is for people with the disorder to receive proper, personalized treatment. When dealing with uncontrollable impulses, anything can happen. This is what makes treatment for bipolar disorder so crucial.

Ask a Healthcare Professional

When you or your loved one are ready to consult a professional about the symptoms you have noticed, you should call your primary care physician (PCP). If you don't currently have a PCP, don't worry! Many places will provide resources for you to find help, like urgent care centers. Your health insurance company can also provide a list of mental health professionals in your local area who accept your insurance. Your health insurance company is an excellent resource. You can usually find their customer service phone number and website on the back of your insurance card. A customer service representative can search for providers within your network and geographical area and provide you with a detailed contact list. On your insurance company's website, you may also be able to search for mental health providers using specific filters, like office location, provider specialty, and availability for new clients. For example, you could search for psychiatrists in your area who specialize in bipolar disorder. It may take some research and many phone calls to find the right provider for your situation, but it will all be worth it to be able to treat your symptoms.

If you choose to seek help from your PCP or a different medical practitioner, they may then refer you to a psychiatrist or psychologist to continue your evaluation. Depending on how severe your symptoms are, they can refer you to someone in your network. If your PCP observes symptoms or behaviors that put you at risk of harming yourself or others, they may arrange a more immediate psychiatric appointment for you.

Unfortunately, some doctors may offer to diagnose and treat your symptoms without consulting a mental health specialist. While this is not inherently wrong to do, they should be open about referring you to someone with specific expertise in bipolar disorder treatment. It can be intimidating to question your general practitioner, but you have control over your treatment. Ask for referrals if they are not given to you right away, and do not be afraid to ask your PCP what their experience is in bipolar disorder diagnoses. Your doctor can and should provide you with every resource and answer they can provide.

Deciding who to trust with your mental health is a big decision. As you receive referrals for different therapists and psychiatrists, research their specialty areas and experience. Most, if not all, mental health professionals will have online information about who they are, where they received their education, and which areas of expertise they specialize in. While there are many qualified professionals in the field of psychology, only a handful will be a perfect fit for you. During the beginning stages of research, look for someone who has experience with diagnosing and treating bipolar disorder. It may also be important to you to see someone of a specific gender or age, which is a valid condition. Sometimes, you're just more comfortable with someone who can relate to your lifestyle, instead of someone from a different background or gender experience.

In the event that you are overwhelmed with decisions, asking people you trust about their experiences may help. Someone, or multiple people, in your inner circle have likely dealt with similar issues. They may recommend a mental health professional that suits your needs. It may also be a pleasant surprise to connect with someone you trust about receiving mental health treatment. You truly never know who has experience with what you're going through until you ask. Beginning this journey of mental well-being may also be overwhelming to go through on your own. If the process becomes too much to do by yourself, consider asking a close friend or family member to help you do research and conduct phone calls with potential providers. Doing so can lessen the weight on your shoulders and form a stronger bond with your loved one. They will probably feel honored that you trust them to help with something so important!

When it is time to meet with a psychiatrist or therapist for an initial evaluation, prepare yourself for the appointment by writing down any symptoms or behaviors that are of particular concern for you. Moreover, it will help to understand the difference between the professionals you are seeking treatment from. A psychologist is a formal title for someone with a degree in Psychology. Many psychologists work as therapists, though there are some who focus on research and academia. Licensed Mental Health Counselors (LMHC) work with an advanced degree in counseling, also known as therapy. It is likely that any therapist you see will be licensed as a mental health counselor.

Finally, there are psychiatrists. These are people who have spent as many as 12 years studying mental health, medicine, and counseling. Psychiatrists go through medical school after receiving their undergraduate degree in order to specialize in diagnosing and prescribing medications for mental illnesses. These doctors typically specialize in certain fields, so you will most likely be able to find a psychiatrist who can directly treat your bipolar disorder. To be prescribed medication, a doctor must be the one to recommend the drug. This can either be your PCP or a psychiatrist. If you choose to see an LMHC, or therapist, they will refer you to a psychiatrist for an additional evaluation to determine your eligibility for medication. Going this route may be the best way to receive the right medication for your specific type of bipolar disorder.

One last step you can take when choosing a provider is to look at reviews made by their previous clients. Some counseling services have websites that include client testimonials, which can be invaluable in your search. However, take any reviews you find with a grain of salt. Only you can decide who is truly a good fit for you, but reading about other people's experiences can help you make that decision.

Prepare for Your Appointment

You already know that it is important to prepare for your first appointment with a mental health expert or bipolar disorder specialist. Going into the appointment with any questions or concerns that you have is a fantastic start. Additionally, try to bring as much information as you can about your medical history, as well as any family history of mental illness. The psychiatrist or therapist may also ask about any medications you may be currently taking, so keep track of the names and doses that you take.

If you received a referral from your doctor for a psychiatrist or therapist, they most likely sent over your medical evaluation and health history. This is great because it can give the mental health specialist a good idea of what concerns you expressed, along with your PCP's professional medical opinion.

In addition to asking about your symptoms, a mental health specialist will typically ask when your symptoms started and if they have gotten better or worse over time. It's okay if you don't remember specific dates or times, but it can help to have somewhat of an idea of when you first noticed your symptoms or troubling behaviors. Maybe they began around the same time as an important event or moment in your life. Knowing what happened around the time your symptoms began can assist you in remembering when they first started.

Thriveworks, a website designed to provide mental health treatment and advice, provides great examples of questions you may want to ask your psychiatrist and therapist. Asking what types of therapies they commonly use to treat bipolar disorder, how the process of choosing a medication works, and if you will be involved in establishing your treatment plan are just a few examples provided by the site.

Overall, you'll be asked and will ask a lot of questions about your health. Be as open and honest as you can with your doctors. It can be nerve-wracking to unload such personal information onto a relative stranger, but know that they are not here to judge you. Mental health experts are usually very passionate about their work and want to help people just like you. They should feel like a safe person to whom you can talk about your personal problems and worries with. If they do not feel safe and comfortable, they may not be the right provider for you.

KNOW YOUR TREATMENT OPTIONS

There are several treatment options at your disposal, so take advantage of them if you can! Medications, therapies, and support groups have been proven to reduce the intensity of bipolar disorder symptoms, making it easier for people to perform daily tasks and maintain relationships. For many people with bipolar disorder, a combination of treatments can be the most effective course of action. By now, you already know the different doctors and mental health experts that can be part of your treatment team. The next step is understanding exactly how certain treatments work and what impacts they can have on your life.

Medications for Bipolar Disorder

With your psychiatrist's guidance, take the time to research medications commonly used to treat bipolar disorder. There are many prescription drugs to choose from, ranging from mood stabilizers to anti-anxiety medications. Your psychiatrist will be able to narrow down which prescriptions will interact safely with your symptoms, health conditions, and any additional medication you may take.

Each medication used to treat bipolar disorder is unique. They all have their own benefits and risks, and your body may react more severely to some than to others. Keeping track of your medications and symptoms consistently is a great way to stay on top of your mental health. Note any symptom changes or side effects you feel once you start a new prescription, including physical changes like weight gain, rapid heartbeat, or headaches. Tell your psychiatrist at your next appointment of any side effects you've noticed since starting your medication, even if you do not believe they are significant.

There is a common misconception that you can stop taking medications when you feel better; however, this is not the case. If you are taking medications prescribed by your doctor or psychiatrist, do not take less or more than what is recommended; and do not stop taking them without first consulting an expert. Feeling better means your medication is working, but it does not mean the battle with bipolar disorder is officially over. Be patient with your treatment, stay consistent, and speak with a professional whenever you have questions or concerns about your meds.

Mood Stabilizers

According to the symptoms that are most prevalent in your experience with bipolar disorder, some medications will be more effective than others. If you struggle with mania or hypomania, your psychiatrist may prescribe a mood stabilizer. This type of medication helps regulate feelings of mania and hypomania, causing episodes to be less severe and frequent. You may have heard of some mood stabilizers; Depakote, Lithobid, Depakene, Tegretol, Equetro, and Lamictal are often prescribed for those who experience manic or hypomanic episodes. If you are prescribed a mood stabilizer for your bipolar disorder, keep in mind that it may take a few weeks or longer for the medicine to take effect. Additionally, you and your psychiatrist will need to keep a close eye on any symptom changes while you are on medication. It may be necessary to adjust the dose or type of medication, depending on how your body reacts.

Antipsychotics

Another common type of medication that treats bipolar disorder symptoms is an antipsychotic. Try not to let the name intimidate you—antipsychotics are simply more effective drugs used to lessen symptoms that are too strong for mood stabilizers. Common antipsychotics include Zyprexa, Abilify, Latuda, and Seroquel. These drugs can be prescribed on their own or in combination with certain bipolar disorder medications. Your psychiatrist will determine if an antipsychotic, or combination, is needed to treat your symptoms. This will typically happen after you have already tried a mood stabilizer on its own, with little to no effect on your symptoms.

Antidepressants

On top of mood stabilizers and antipsychotics, your psychiatrist may prescribe an antidepressant if you are struggling with depressive episodes. As with the first two medications you have read about, antidepressants may be used in combination with other bipolar treatments. According to the Mayo Clinic (2021b), antidepressants have the potential to cause manic or hypomanic episodes, due to their ability to raise a person's mood. This means that the use of antidepressants for bipolar disorder must be closely monitored to ensure the user's safety. The benefits and risks of using antidepressants for bipolar disorder are still being weighed by researchers and psychiatrists, so there is no clear answer on whether or not this type of medication is most effective (WebMD, 2022b).

Other Medications

There are medications being developed to treat depression and manic episodes at the same time. One medication, called Symbyax, has been approved as an antidepressant-antipsychotic. For those who experience anxiety as a symptom of their bipolar disorder, as-needed medications are sometimes prescribed. These drugs, known as benzodiazepines, are recommended for limited and short-term use, mainly to treat panic attacks. Common names for benzodiazepines are Xanax, Klonopin, and Valium. Always consult your psychiatrist before attempting to take these types of medications, as they are known for being highly addictive and habit-forming.

Bear in mind that drinking alcohol while taking bipolar disorder medications is not recommended. Consuming alcohol while on certain medications can result in dangerous side effects. At the very least, you can experience dizziness, drowsiness, and slowed breathing. At the most, you can severely damage your liver, induce tremors and depressive symptoms, and cause injury to yourself or others. Being responsible for your health means taking your treatment seriously. You will not only feel better, but you will avoid any future illnesses or injuries.

Therapies and Support Groups

Whether you take medication for your bipolar disorder or not, therapy can alleviate the many emotional symptoms you feel. Your psychiatrist can refer you to therapists who specialize in treating bipolar disorder and depression, granting you access to an invaluable resource. Speaking with someone who knows what you are going through and is unbiased, meaning they only know what you tell them about yourself, can lessen the emotional burden that comes with mental illness.

Therapy involves more than just sitting in a comfy chair and talking to a counselor. Granted, talking is a huge component of attending therapy, but it is not the only part. There are several types of therapy that can treat your bipolar disorder symptoms, including cognitive behavioral therapy (CBT), dialectical behavior therapy (DBT), family-focused therapy (FFT), and more.

Cognitive Behavioral Therapy

CBT focuses on your individual experience with bipolar disorder. In CBT sessions, you will identify the negative habits and thought processes that come as a result of your symptoms and learn to create new, healthier habits and thoughts. Typically, CBT sessions are one-on-one and involve developing strategies with your therapist that will help you stay positive during depressive episodes and level-headed during manic episodes.

Dialectical Behavior Therapy

Similarly to cognitive behavioral therapy, DBT is a type of therapy that encourages the development of mindfulness skills. DBT can be performed in both individual and group settings and teaches clients ways to view their bipolar symptoms from an objective stance. Essentially, DBT shows those with bipolar disorder how to observe their thoughts, emotions, and physical reactions without self-criticism. People who attend DBT are taught how to accept themselves and their bipolar symptoms.

Interpersonal and Social Rhythm Therapy

Interpersonal and social rhythm therapy, IPSRT, focuses on establishing routines and identifying the consequences of routine adjustments. A person with bipolar disorder who attends IPSRT sessions will keep track of their daily routines, such as sleep and meal times, and develop a structure that promotes wellness.

The therapist may also help their client identify inter-personal problem areas in their life, like relationship or friendship conflicts, in order to come up with solutions for the future. This works to stabilize the person's mood and prevent further problems in their relationships.

Family-Focused Therapy

Family-Focused therapy is just as it sounds: focused on the family. FFT consists of a number of sessions where a bipolar person and their loved ones attend together. There are many different types of family units, including spouses and partners, parents and children, and siblings. All of these types can benefit from trying FFT with their bipolar loved one.

FFT involves educating a person and their support system about bipolar disorder, ranging from the diagnosis process to different treatment methods. The therapist will encourage the group to ask questions, communicate honestly about their feelings, and work on solving family conflicts that are caused by bipolar disorder symptoms. The family will spend multiple sessions working as a team and developing strategies that will benefit everyone involved in a bipolar person's healing process.

Internal Family Systems

Internal Family Systems, also known as IFS, is a newer type of psychotherapy that combines the ideals of family-focused therapy with inner self-reflection. Guided by their therapists, clients address inner "sub-personalities" and identify their roles within the body and mind (Schwartz, 2023). The main goal of IFS is for the client to connect with all parts of themselves, both positive and negative, and treat each one equally. Each subpersonality is viewed as a good part of "the self," even if it is initially perceived as bad. The client is tasked with befriending each of their subpersonalities and tending to their specific needs. In general, IFS promotes self-compassion, inner child work, and trauma healing.

Psychoeducation

Rather than a typical sit-down therapy session, psychoeducation is more like a class. Everyone in attendance, no matter how large the group is, will be educated on bipolar disorder. Some psychoeducation classes may focus on sharing personal stories, while others may consist of an educational structure and agenda. Sometimes, it can be a combination of both methods. The purpose of psychoeducation for treating bipolar disorder is to destigmatize the condition and learn how it truly works. It also provides a supportive community for those who are struggling with their diagnosis and symptoms.

With 21st century technology and social structures, therapy and psychoeducation are more accessible than ever. If you have access to the internet, you probably have access to a therapy session. There are various websites and platforms that provide psychological and psychiatric interventions for people struggling with mental illness. Today, a client has the ability to communicate with their therapist through email, instant messaging, phone calls, and video chats. This method is often called telehealth.

The onset of the Covid-19 pandemic caused a significant increase in telehealth appointments. Doctors, therapists, and psychiatrists began using virtual methods of communication when their clients were unable to go into an office. This was, and still is, a handy tool for anyone who is quarantined in their home, struggles in public social settings, or lives in a rural area with limited access to mental health services. If you feel that telehealth or virtual appointments could benefit you, speak to your providers about the many available possibilities.

Alternative Treatments

Treating bipolar disorder is not solely about taking medication or going to therapy. While these are highly beneficial for many people, they are not the only options for someone looking for help. There are various alternative treatments and lifestyle adjustments that are believed to help people with bipolar disorder.

Some research suggests that herbal nutrients, supplements, and certain vitamins can aid in managing bipolar disorder symptoms. Fatty acids found in fish oil are said to reduce symptoms of depression, such as irritability and aggression (Healthline, 2019). These acids, known as Omega-3 fatty acids, may also improve brain function. Other supplements, like *S*-adenosylmethionine, *N*-acetylcysteine, and *Rhodiola rosea* are thought to decrease feelings of depression and mania. Vitamins like melatonin, choline, and inositol also show benefits in studies regarding bipolar disorder. Additionally, some people believe Chinese herbs and medicinal cannabis relieve symptoms of bipolar disorder, though this has not been sufficiently studied by researchers (NeuRA Library, n.d.). Remember, any supplement, vitamin, or herb you consider taking should be discussed with your healthcare providers.

Healthy Lifestyles

If supplements don't appeal to you, you can find help in other ways. The following methods are fantastic for lifting your spirits and promoting overall wellness, though they should not be relied on as a sole treatment method.

Exercise has been proven time and time again to increase endorphins, making people feel happier. For depressive and hypomanic symptoms of bipolar disorder, exercise can be a great pick-me-up and sleep aid. Moving your body can even reduce the anxiety that stems from concerns about one's bipolar disorder diagnosis.

However, for people who experience manic episodes, exercise can possibly make symptoms worse. An article published by Healthline (2019) mentions a study that found a decrease in anxiety and depression for people with bipolar disorder who exercised regularly. Yet, in the same study, it was reported that exercise caused more manic symptoms in those going through a manic episode. The rush of energy and endorphins may cause a spiraling effect, meaning that people with bipolar I may not benefit from regular exercise in the same way as those with other types of bipolar disorder (Wells, 2019). Be sure to check in with your doctor if you experience any adverse reactions to exercise, especially in regard to your bipolar disorder symptoms.

Creating a balanced lifestyle can help the symptoms that are worsened by exercise or other stimulants. Eating well and hydrating your body will encourage better mood regulation and consistent energy levels. Studies have shown that there are specific foods that promote brain and body health. Fish, berries, nuts, and seeds all have the potential to lower your risk of depression (Davidson, 2020). Bananas, oats, yogurt, dark chocolate, and even coffee are also known to be good mood boosters. Of course, our moods can be affected by various factors, especially when bipolar disorder is considered. Nonetheless, indulging in these healthy foods will most likely help your body and mind in more ways than one. In the same vein, drinking plenty of water and staying hydrated throughout the day can help stabilize moods and reduce tension and feelings of depression (Stanborough, 2020).

Developing consistent sleeping schedules and spending time outdoors are also good ways to avoid intense depression. As you can probably imagine, not getting enough quality sleep can result in days full of irritation and high tempers. It's not fun to feel tired when you should be feeling energized, especially when your mood depends on it. The relationship between sleep and your mood is cyclical, meaning that your mood affects your sleep in the same way that sleep affects your mood. When you get consistent, good-quality sleep, you are likely to feel better during the day. Feeling better during the day will, in turn, promote a better night's sleep. If you are experiencing depression, anxiety, or mania during the day, it can make your sleep patterns become unpredictable, or nonexistent.

Connecting with nature can also make you feel happier in times of stress or depression. It does not matter if you live in a busy city or a lush forest; you can find the beauty of nature anywhere. If you are lucky enough to live in a place that is full of greenery and biodiversity, take advantage! Explore your area and observe the many wonders nature can provide. If you live in a place that has limited pockets of foliage and greenery, try to acknowledge the more subtle wonders. Birds chirping, leaves blowing in the wind, and flowers growing in unexpected places can remind you how beautiful life can be, even when it is more difficult to see. Let the natural world around you bring you a sense of peace.

Calming Rituals and Routines

Establishing calming rituals in your daily life can not only provide you with a sense of control over your well-being, but a pleasant predictability, too. Rituals can be whatever you want them to be, from a simple morning routine to a multi-step plan you enact every day. Meditations, stretches, breathing techniques, and more have been shown to reduce anxiety and stress.

Researchers have found that certain exercises and movements can release stored tension in the body, typically occurring as a result of stress and trauma. Tension and trauma-releasing exercises, known as TRE®, have been developed in the hopes that more people can find healing by regulating their nervous systems. TRE® is described as "an innovative series of exercises that assist the body in releasing deep muscular patterns of stress, tension, and trauma" (Trauma Prevention, n.d.). The exercises are typically taught by an instructor and activate specific muscles. The developers of TRE® claim that those who practice the exercises feel an overall sense of wellness, calm, and balance afterward.

In addition to TRE®, you can incorporate mental and breathing exercises into your daily routine. Harvard University has published a list of relaxation techniques that they have found to help reduce stress and increase feelings of peace. The techniques include: focusing on taking slow, deep breaths while clearing the mind; body scanning, which means focusing on relaxing parts of your body one by one; imagining calming, positive imagery; practicing mindfulness by focusing on how you feel in the present moment; performing yoga, tai chi, and qigong exercises; and repeating affirmations, prayers, or mantras while focusing on breathing steadily (Harvard, 2022). These relaxation techniques can be practiced in any order or combination. What matters most is that you do what works best for you.

Another breathing technique that many people use to reduce anxiety in their daily life is called "box breathing." While it may seem obvious that breathing is important, a lot of people do not realize that there are certain ways of breathing that promote certain benefits. Box breathing involves taking a deep breath in for four seconds, holding it for four seconds, exhaling for four seconds, and resting naturally for four seconds. This pattern brings your attention to your breathing, allowing you to release any intrusive or repetitive thoughts.

It can help to imagine each set of four seconds as a side of a square box, hence the name of the technique. In chapter seven, you can find more detailed instructions for box breathing and other techniques, like meditating and repeating affirmations.

Sensory distraction activities may also be a beneficial addition to your daily rituals and routines. There are countless ways to distract yourself during an anxious or stressful time. Some ways include cuddling your beloved pet, using a weighted blanket or vest, squeezing a stress ball, and blowing bubbles. Distracting your senses when you are feeling overwhelmed or restless can help focus your attention and bring you peace. It's possible that you already practice sensory distraction in your life without even realizing it! Simply taking deep breaths or sitting in a warm bubble bath can be considered sensory calming activities.

Another type of sensory calming activity is acting on your creative instincts. Maybe you enjoy using adult coloring books or making collages. Perhaps you find joy in painting or making music. Whatever it is that expresses your creativity is something that should absolutely be included in your daily routine. Being creative has been scientifically proven to induce feelings of happiness and optimism (Brenner, 2019). Even a quick five-minute art or music session can help alleviate depression and anxiety, especially for people struggling with depressive episodes associated with bipolar disorder.

MONITORING YOUR SYMPTOMS

Understanding your moods and behavioral patterns can help you better understand your overall experience with bipolar disorder, thus making it easier for you to manage your symptoms. Once you know what helps your symptoms and what makes them worse, you can plan your routines accordingly to avoid future conflicts.

There are several ways you can track your symptoms and moods. One easy way is to keep a daily journal in which you report the symptoms and moods you experience each day. If you attend therapy sessions, you can bring this journal up to your therapist and go over any patterns or notable moments that you have recorded. You and your therapist can then develop a healthy routine based on your findings.

If journaling seems like too big of an undertaking, there are various mood-tracking apps and worksheets that you may like. The Depression and Bipolar Support Alliance has developed an in-depth Wellness Tracker that can be downloaded straight from the DBSA website. This tracker enables you to create a color-coded chart of your specific emotions and symptoms, as well as provides a journal section for your daily experiences. All you have to do is print the tracker, mark which symptoms you had and when, and write yourself a quick note about your day.

There are also many apps for your phone and computer that allow you to record your symptoms and moods. Some apps require a small payment, while others are free to download. Some noteworthy apps, as mentioned by BPHope (2017), are iMoodJournal, Bipolar Mood Tracker, eMoods, MindDoc, Moodnotes, and Daylio. I encourage you to explore each application to see which, if any, feels right for you. You can find links to each of these apps in chapter eight.

Just remember: treating your bipolar disorder is a large task that requires determination and self-reliance. However, you do not have to do it alone. You have the ability to establish a wonderful team of family, friends, and healthcare professionals to support you on your healing journey.

Key Takeaway:

Although bipolar disorder does not yet have a cure, there is a variety of treatment methods and symptom management for those with a diagnosis. Leaving your bipolar disorder untreated can lead to a plethora of social, mental, and physical challenges; so it is imperative to work with medical professionals to create a treatment plan that works best for you. Prescription medications, therapy, holistic approaches, and lifestyle adjustments are just a few of the many ways to live a successful life with bipolar disorder. When you are able to monitor and manage your symptoms, you are able to thrive.

IT TAKES A VILLAGE

> *A generous heart is always open, always ready to receive our going and coming. In the midst of such love, we need never fear abandonment. This is the most precious gift true love offers—the experience of knowing we always belong.*

> — BELL HOOKS

COMMUNICATING ABOUT YOUR BIPOLAR EXPERIENCE

The people you consistently surround yourself with are usually the people who will make up your support system. Friends, close family members, medical professionals, therapists, and even colleagues can be members of your team. As long as they are someone you trust and can confide in, they may be able to help in one way or another. Friends and family can offer you support at home or in social situations by recognizing the warning signs of depressive and manic episodes and offering you a safe place to feel your intense emotions. Doctors and therapists can provide you with resources, answers to your questions, and unbiased perspectives to help ground you in moments of stress or frustration. At work or in school, colleagues and peers that are aware of your condition can help you feel less alone, or even assist you in getting out of triggering situations without attracting unwanted attention. However, the only way for your team to know what to do in such circumstances is for you to communicate with them.

In order to establish a solid support system, you must be able to communicate about your experience with bipolar disorder. This means expressing your true thoughts and feelings to your loved ones and doctors, instead of trying to make things sound more manageable than they really are. The people that make up your support system will be there for you unconditionally and will never judge you for what you feel. Being authentic in your communication about your disorder will allow your team to support you in the exact ways you need and want.

Learn How to Open Up and Ask for Support

You may feel uncomfortable asking for help with your bipolar disorder, especially if you are used to handling things on your own. It's important to remind yourself that asking for help is not a sign of weakness, but rather one of strength. It takes courage and confidence to open up about things that are causing you pain. It is only as uncomfortable as you make it—if you open the conversation with self-acceptance and understanding, you will most likely feel less unsure about the discussion.

Of course, if you are feeling the depressive symptoms of bipolar disorder, you may be more hesitant to ask for help. Depression can cause you to want to retreat from relationships, particularly the ones you care most about. Feeling depressed can mean feeling low levels of self-esteem and self-worth, which makes it a challenge to speak to loved ones about your negative feelings. You may feel that, by talking about your problems, you are burdening your family and friends with negativity. It's likely that you are also feeling so down on yourself that you think it's useless to try and communicate your emotions, assuming they cannot be alleviated. Fortunately, your negative thoughts and feelings *can* be alleviated by communicating with people you trust. The simple act of speaking your feelings aloud can lessen the weight on your shoulders.

Wherever your hesitation to ask for help stems from—be it feeling embarrassed, weak, or burdensome—know that there are people out there willing to do whatever they can for you. If your hesitation is strong enough that you convince yourself to suffer in silence, try to reframe your perspective on seeking help from others.

Clinical psychologist Debbie Sorensen has published her recommended techniques for changing your view on the subject. In an article for Psyche, a mental wellness website, Sorensen reminds readers that "it's important to examine any thoughts or beliefs that might be getting in your way" (2022). Begin by addressing any assumptions you have about asking for help. Does the idea hold negative connotations for you? That is, do you feel that seeking help makes you lazy, needy, or too dependent on others? If so, explore what has made you feel this way, such as a past experience or comment someone made once that stuck with you.

Similarly, do your negative associations with the idea of asking for help stem from a place of self-criticism or insecurity? Take a moment to decide whether you find it more beneficial to adhere to limiting self-beliefs or to make positive changes for your well-being. Sorensen also discusses the importance of being vulnerable. She puts forward the idea that allowing yourself to open up to others, especially about such serious topics, can establish a deeper connection between you and the people you love (Sorenson, 2022).

The article describes various ways to actually ask for help, in addition to getting yourself more comfortable with the task. Using assertive communication, instead of aggressive or passive communication, will avoid any miscommunications or missed opportunities. When you are seeking help from someone, Sorensen suggests being clear and direct about what you need from them. You do not need to demand their action or assistance, nor should you be so unclear that the other person is unsure how to help. Understand how the person can help and tell them what they can do if they are willing and able. More than likely, they will appreciate your honesty and respect that you sought them out specifically for their abilities. If they do agree to help you, allow yourself to feel relief and gratitude. If they decline, albeit respectfully, try not to dwell on any negative thoughts. Just because they are unable to assist you how you need right now, doesn't mean they will be unwilling or unable to help in the future. If you would like to access the full article by Debbie Sorensen, titled *How to Ask for Help*, visit www.psyche.co/guides/how-to-ask-for-help-without-discomfort-or-apology.

If you are still hesitant about asking your loved ones and peers for help, that's okay. It takes time to feel comfortable enough to be vulnerable, even more so when you are dealing with something as serious as bipolar disorder. Be patient with yourself and your needs. If you are able to communicate with your doctor or therapist, see if they can offer any guidance about approaching the subject with your family and friends. They have most likely had similar questions from other clients and will provide you with good advice.

Educate Your Loved Ones About Bipolar Disorder

Sometimes, despite their best efforts, it can be difficult for members of your support system to fully understand what you are going through. They may not have experience with mental illness or helping someone through such a tough time, but that does not mean they are incapable of supporting you. In this case, if you believe this person will truly make a positive difference in your treatment, it is your responsibility to help them understand your experience.

It would be a huge relief if everyone in your life knew all there is to know about bipolar disorder. Yet, this is not a reality for most people. Some of your loved ones or peers may have experience with the disorder, whether they have been diagnosed themselves or have known someone who has. Others, though, may have a limited understanding of bipolar disorder, mostly stemming from what they have observed in films and on television. A lot of the time, this type of understanding can lead to the harmful stereotypes and misconceptions that were mentioned in chapter two. For the members of your support system who have little to no knowledge about the disorder, you can be their educator.

Learning How Bipolar Disorder Affects Relationships

The first step your loved ones can take is to learn from this book, which will introduce them to the many ideas and facts they should know about bipolar disorder. The fifth, seventh, and eighth chapters, in particular, were written to provide practical solutions and valuable resources for anyone affected by the disorder. Secondly, it will benefit both you and members of your support system to know what to expect from a relationship in which one, or more than one, person has bipolar disorder.

When bipolar disorder is present in a romantic relationship, it can be challenging to keep track of the frequent changes in physical intimacy. During manic or hypomanic episodes, it is common for a bipolar person to feel more driven by sexual desires. They may talk about or initiate sex more often than when they are not feeling symptoms of mania (Payne, n.d.). On the other end of the intimacy spectrum, depressive episodes can consist of long periods without any sexual intimacy. For the person with bipolar disorder, avoiding physical intimacy may be common when they are depressed. This unpredictable fluctuation of sexual desire can be confusing for both partners. If you are part of a romantic relationship that is affected by bipolar disorder, be sure to remind yourself that fluctuating intimacy is to be expected.

For families affected by bipolar disorder, erratic and unpredictable moods can cause a significant strain on the family unit. Children with bipolar parents may feel confused by their constant changes in mood, as well as the unexpected behaviors that occur. It's crucial to discuss the reality of the condition with children so that they can feel as safe and supported as possible within their families. It may be necessary to tailor the discussion to the child's ability to understand, depending on their age and developmental level. You may not need to go into too much detail if the child is young; simply explaining that their parent experiences certain changes to their mood, but is receiving treatment, can make the situation much less confusing.

Educating Your Team About Your Experience

Everyone's experience with bipolar disorder is unique, so teaching your support system about your personal journey and symptoms is key. While it can be good for them to know about the general patterns and behaviors associated with the disorder, it is most important for your loved ones to know what bipolar disorder is like for *you*. Teach your support system about the symptoms you experience most frequently, in addition to the behaviors you tend to exhibit.

If you are actively attending therapy sessions, you may be aware of certain triggers and warning signs that are associated with your bipolar disorder. Explain to your loved ones that depressive and manic episodes can be exacerbated by specific situations and discuss which triggers affect you the most. You can also teach your support system how to recognize when an episode is beginning. Warning signs of a depressive episode include feeling sad, hopeless, or irritable more often than not; lacking energy or motivation; finding it difficult to concentrate; feeling pessimistic; and expressing feelings of guilt, shame, or self-doubt. Manic or hypomanic episodes tend to show early signs, as well, such as erratic behavior, bursts of energy, and excessive talking. Teaching your support system how to identify these behaviors early on can help them cope with your episodes and gain a better understanding of how they start.

Educating your support system also involves explaining which treatments you have tried and are currently trying. The responsibility of maintaining treatments can be heavy, but the burden can be eased with help from your team. Your loved ones can assist you in managing your medications and appointment schedules so that you can worry less and focus on healing. If you have developed specific lifestyle habits and routines that help you manage your symptoms, explain them to your support team. Acknowledge the importance of keeping up with your routines and allow your loved ones to help you complete them if needed.

Last, but not least, educate your team of supporters on what is helpful to say to someone with bipolar disorder —along with what is not. Questions like "how are you?" and "what can I do to help you today?" show that a person truly cares. On the contrary, asking why a bipolar person is acting "crazy" or if they can "snap out" of their mood can cause them to feel ashamed, misunderstood, and frustrated. Telling a bipolar person to calm down or relax, particularly when they are feeling severely manic or depressed, can be just as harmful. If it were that easy to feel at peace, surely it would be done right away.

Overall, encouraging your support system to be compassionate and forgiving will make a positive impact on your treatment. Your friends, family, and trusted peers should try not to take your behaviors or moods personally, as bipolar disorder makes it difficult to regulate your emotions. Similarly, you should communicate honestly and empathetically with your support team. Listen to their concerns and understand how your bipolar disorder affects them, just as they have listened to you. It is crucial to create a safe, comforting space within your team.

Take Care of Your Physical and Emotional Needs

Whether you are someone with bipolar disorder or part of your loved one's support system, it's essential to take care of your own needs. For the person with bipolar disorder, maintaining overall wellness is a must. For their supporters and caregivers, this is also necessary. There is a well-known saying that you can't help anyone if you don't help yourself first. Think about being on an airplane. Before takeoff, the crew always emphasizes the importance of putting your oxygen mask on before helping someone else put their's on. This idea is the same for helping someone with mental illness. Caring for and supporting a loved one can only be successful if you are able to avoid feeling burnt out and overwhelmed.

Support Groups and Therapy

Attending support groups or networks can give you space to vent and find clarity when you are struggling with the treatment process. There are so many different ways to connect with the bipolar community, many of which you can easily find online. Websites for NAMI (the National Alliance on Mental Illness) and SAMHSA (the Substance Abuse and Mental Health Services Administration) provide invaluable resources for those looking for support. On these sites, you will find phone numbers for mental health hotlines, links to treatment centers, and different support groups you can join.

Support groups are beneficial for everyone impacted by bipolar disorder. People with the disorder can join groups with their peers to discuss their personal experiences, as well as gain inspiration and support from one another. Families and loved ones of a bipolar person can also find support groups, in which they can do the same. Connecting with others who have similar experiences with bipolar disorder is a surefire way to feel more confident about your role as a supporter of someone with the condition.

Members of someone's support system may also benefit from therapy, in the same way that someone with bipolar disorder would. Individual and group therapy can provide a safe space for your loved ones to express any concerns, frustration, or overwhelming feelings without causing conflict in their personal relationships.

For your convenience, links to the organizations mentioned above—as well as other helpful websites, hotlines, and educational books—are included in chapter eight.

Healthy Boundaries

Another great way to keep everyone involved while staying positive and engaged is to set clear boundaries.

Boundaries are the guidelines and limitations you give to others in order to receive the respect and consideration you deserve. You can set boundaries about virtually anything. You don't like when someone enters your bedroom or office without knocking first? A perfect boundary to set would be to tell them they have to knock and wait for permission to enter your space. Do you get uncomfortable when people complain about personal problems without seeing if it's an okay time to do so? Set a boundary by telling them you can only support their venting when *you* have the emotional capacity for it, so they need to check in with you first before unloading their problems onto you.

Boundaries are a practice of self-confidence and compassion. When you set a boundary with someone, it should not be your intention to boss them around or dictate their every action. Instead, setting a boundary is a way for you to maintain your relationships in a way that feels healthy and manageable. The idea of boundary-setting is mutual, too. If you can confidently set a boundary that will be respected by someone, they should be able to do the same with you, within reason. Respect goes both ways.

When it comes to bipolar disorder, boundaries are fantastic tools. Frequent mood changes can lead to frequent misunderstandings and frustrations, especially when someone's support system is unaware of a mood shift. When someone is in a manic episode, they may be more open to conversations and treatment practices. However, because many people with bipolar disorder transition from mania to depression every few weeks, their openness to communicate and receive help can fluctuate unexpectedly. What they once accepted from loved ones as help may suddenly feel overbearing, or even annoying, when they are depressed.

Setting boundaries for these times can help. If you are the person receiving treatment for bipolar disorder, try to observe your thoughts and emotions in times when you are feeling overwhelmed or pessimistic. Take note of any specific interactions that upset you and try to understand why. Many times, we become upset when people fail to honor our values or what is most important to us. Make a mental or physical list of what you value most in the world. Ideas, emotions, interactions—these can all play into your values. When you are clear on what you find important, it can be easier to recognize when someone's actions or words negatively impact you.

Once you know your values, you can begin to set boundaries based on them. Boundaries can be flexible and should be adjusted whenever your values, knowledge, or desires change. Do not be afraid to tell your family, friends, or even your doctors about the boundaries you would like to put in place. As your support system, they should make an effort to understand where you are coming from and do their best to respect your wishes.

Similarly, members of your support team can set boundaries with you. There may be instances in which your bipolar symptoms caused you to say or do something that hurts a loved one. It happens to the best of us. When this occurs, allow your loved ones to set boundaries with you. They may ask you to let them know when you feel like you are in a depressive or manic episode so that they can be more conscious of how they speak to you to avoid conflict. Members of your support team may also set boundaries that give them time away from the situation. In heated moments, such as an argument or during displays of erratic behavior, it can help everyone to take some time for themselves to regroup.

Saying "no" or "that does not work for me" is always an acceptable response if it benefits your well-being. For everyone involved in your treatment, using boundaries to maintain the health of their relationships is a necessary skill.

If one of your boundaries is ignored, it can leave you feeling upset and disrespected. Unfortunately, you cannot force someone to act differently. All you can do in the situation is explain to them how their lack of respect makes you feel and ask why they chose to ignore your boundary in the first place. There are many possible reasons why someone would disrespect your boundary: they may have forgotten and acted without thinking; they may feel that the boundary is too rigid or unrealistic; or they may simply not care. While the latter option can be painful to realize, the first two possibilities have the potential to be worked on.

In the event that someone forgot about your boundary, take the time to explain it to them clearly and directly. It may be a boundary they are not used to, causing them to need more time to understand how to respect it. Having patience in this particular situation will benefit both you and the other person.

When someone ignores a boundary because they feel it is too rigid or unrealistic, try to open up an honest conversation about the subject. In addition to finding out why it feels unachievable for the other person, ask yourself if there is any room for negotiation. As previously mentioned, some boundaries can be flexible enough to adjust without serious repercussions. Identify how strongly you feel about the specific boundary and see if there are any possible scenarios in which it can be tailored to be mutually beneficial. If it is a boundary that feels too important to adjust, be honest with the other person. They have the right to deny your request, just as you have the right to avoid interacting with them if you feel it is going to harm your mental health. Hopefully, however, you both can reach a common ground and find a way to have a healthy relationship.

Honest and Compassionate Feedback

Giving honest feedback is another way for family, friends, and colleagues to support their loved ones with bipolar disorder. Although it may feel easier to tell your loved one that they are doing great even if it's untrue, it will be more beneficial to tell them the truth in a kind and compassionate way. If you notice that the person you care about is exhibiting harmful behaviors or causing unnecessary conflict because of their disorder, it is best to tell them what you have observed. Turning a blind eye to negative behaviors can result in severe consequences for the person with bipolar disorder and their support system.

More specifically, it is crucial for a support team to acknowledge any signs or symptoms of substance abuse. People with bipolar disorder may be introduced to substances, like prescription medications that are highly addictive, or turn to alcohol or drugs as a way of escaping from their reality. Having bipolar disorder does not necessarily mean a person will experience substance abuse, but it does increase their risk of developing dangerous habits (Juergens, 2022). If you observe any concerning behaviors that may be linked to substance abuse, be sure to address them sooner rather than later.

According to Dr. Tanya Chase, Psy.D., a psychologist who works in the San Francisco and specializes in addiction treatment and behavioral health, many people with bipolar disorder do not recognize that they have the disorder. It is often friends and family who first point out the problem and suggest getting help. The friends and family become a reality check for the person with bipolar disorder. It is important to keep these friends and family nearby to give honest feedback about what they observe. Oftentimes, the highest form of love is giving honest feedback with kindness, instead of pretending a problem doesn't exist.

It is important to mention that if a person is also showing symptoms of substance abuse, that friends and family are often the first to notice. Again, it is this village of support that is critical for honest feedback about substance use and bipolar symptoms. Twelve-step programs, like Alcoholics Anonymous, Narcotics Anonymous, Dual-Diagnosis Anonymous, are wonderful communities of support which help people navigate the treatment path for substance use disorders.

BIPOLAR DISORDER SUCCESS STORIES

At this point, you may be feeling overwhelmed with information. You have learned countless facts and figures about bipolar disorder, including how the condition can impact everyone in your life. The wealth of knowledge you currently have is astounding. Regardless of how much valuable information you now have, you may still have concerns about living a life affected by bipolar disorder. If you are a member of a bipolar person's support team, you are probably wondering how you can possibly manage everything while staying positive.

The good news is that people all over the world have seen success with their bipolar treatment. That includes the successes of their support system. An article published on the website for BPHope details the success stories of people helping their loved ones with bipolar disorder. Writer Stephanie Stephens uses her article as a beacon of hope and inspiration, showing that it is entirely possible to have a positive experience with a bipolar loved one (2020). To access the full, online article, visit: https://www.bphope.com/step-by-step-bipolar-success-stories.

Adam's Story

One story mentioned in Stephens' article is that of a man named Adam, who suffered from his bipolar symptoms for a long time before finding the right treatment. When he was in his 20's, Adam experienced various traumas and struggles that led to him discovering his bipolar disorder diagnosis. He was a young husband and father of two children who went through periods of depression and mania. Conflicts arose in his relationships, as well as in his financial situation. Adam spent his money "wildly" and fell into a downward spiral (Stephens, 2020).

Eventually, Adam got injured in a car accident, leading him to become addicted to painkillers. He was in physical pain from his injuries and emotional pain from the deaths of his parents years before. Because he had not yet received a bipolar diagnosis, Adam self-medicated with no clear understanding of his own symptoms. The behaviors associated with his untreated bipolar disorder and substance abuse landed him in the hospital, where his doctors finally gave him a proper diagnosis. Before he was able to use his newfound knowledge for good, Adam spent a few more years getting himself into legal trouble and being alienated from his wife and children.

At last, Adam began to understand that he could work with his bipolar disorder, rather than letting it control his life. He maintained his therapy sessions and proper medication intake, while finding a job designing graphics for his local Mental Health Alliance. It was here that he met a man who became an unconditional member of his support system. This man, named Joe, continuously reached out to Adam, despite the latter's hesitation. Joe knew Adam had the potential to reach great heights and never gave up on him. Over time, Adam and Joe became close friends, with Joe mentoring Adam at the Mental Health Alliance. Adam made a positive name for himself and even used his experience to encourage others suffering in similar circumstances.

Adam is quoted saying "I realized I could take control of my own life", serving as a perfect example of finding success regardless of a bipolar disorder diagnosis (Stephens, 2020).

Kristin's Story

Stephens' article also discusses a woman named Kristin, who spent 25 years allowing her bipolar disorder to dictate her lifestyle before deciding to take control. Kristin was diagnosed with bipolar disorder in the 1980s. She struggled with mood cycling and symptom management, along with the rest of life's obstacles.

After graduating high school, Kristin immediately entered the workforce. She worked multiple jobs, ranging from food services to secretarial work, while raising her son. Because she did not attend college after high school, Kristin felt limited by her lack of a degree or qualifications. On top of that, she was so busy raising her family, working, and managing her mental illness that she had no time to pursue higher education.

Kristin recalls reaching a breaking point in the 1990s, when she realized the opportunities she could have if she had a college degree. She decided to go back to school for a two-year degree in counseling and human services at a local community college. Accomplishing this task proved to Kristin that she could do more, despite her bipolar disorder. The hardworking mother pursued another degree at the University of South Florida, which she attended for four years. In order to be successful in her classes, she knew she would have to find ways to work with her bipolar symptoms, as well as the attention-deficit disorder she had also been diagnosed with.

Kristin spoke with her professors and classmates about her condition and explained that her mood changes may cause her to be absent from class on occasion. She advocated for herself and it paid off. Her classmates were able to fill her in on what lessons she missed and her professors allowed her to take the time off when she needed a break. Kristin found the support she needed to achieve her dreams. By the end of her four years at the university, she graduated with a high grade point average and a bachelor's degree.

Kristin's story closes with an inspiring quote where she emphasizes the fact that bipolar disorder does not have to be the worst thing to happen to you: "Mental illness does not have to diminish your life. It's a huge factor, but it does not mean you cannot have a good, full, contributing life" (Stephens, 2020).

These stories are just a few of the many successes people with bipolar disorder have achieved. With the help of support systems and treatment, you can accomplish anything you put your mind to. If you are a family member or friend of someone with bipolar disorder, know that happy, healthy relationships are possible. If you are a person receiving treatment for bipolar disorder, remember that you have the ability to control your own life. You can and will make it through the darkest parts of your disorder.

Beyond the traditional methods of dealing with this disorder lies a realm where you can find immense hope.

Key Takeaway:

Managing bipolar disorder symptoms and behaviors is a significant undertaking, one that can feel over-whelming without the right support system. For those diagnosed with the disorder, a successful treatment plan depends heavily on having a team of knowledge-able, trustworthy people. This team can include doctors, psychiatrists and therapists, family members, friends, partners, and even co-workers. Your support system should be a safe group of people you can rely on, so that you do not have to manage your mental illness on your own.

The most effective type of support system is one that communicates openly and honestly, sets healthy boundaries, and gives honest but compassionate feed-back. Every member of the group, including the person receiving treatment, must take care of their own phys-ical and emotional needs in order to achieve success as a team.

5

THE FIVE KEYS FOR HOPE™

> *"Let your hopes, not your hurts, shape your future."*
>
> — ROBERT H. SCHULLER

A CATALYST FOR HOPE

I met Kathryn Goetzke in 2010 when she joined a self-development/leadership training I was involved in. I immediately could see in her this beautiful combination of savvy businesswoman/entrepreneur and passionate advocate for destigmatizing depression.

She lost her father to suicide at 18. I've heard her tell the story many times as it was a pivotal and traumatic moment in her life. Kathryn overcame her battles with depression, anxiety, ADHD, PTSD, and addictions through therapy, medication, lifestyle changes, and support. She knows all too well the negative consequences of untreated mental health on both the self and the family system. She has committed her life to helping to support others, not only in the treatment of mental health but in prevention through lifestyle modifications and education.

In honor of her late father, Kathryn started the non-profit iFred (International Foundation for Research and Education on Depression), an organization dedicated to shining a positive light on mental health and eliminating stigma through prevention, research, and education in 2004. iFred has an extensive list of resources on its website as well as education and information about understanding depression.

Through her work and research at iFred, she discovered that one of the key indicators of depression was *hopelessness*. This, in turn, prompted her and a group of experts to create the **Hopeful Minds** program – a free, evidence-based global curriculum to teach hope to kids based on research that hope is a teachable skill. This was then expanded to create **Hopeful Cities**, a marketing plan that operationalizes hope in cities around the world.

She also started a consulting company, Hopeful Mindsets, to focus on college students, adults, and workplaces. She created **Hopeful Mindsets**, an evidence-based course to activate hope on college campuses that any college campus can license, and **SHINE, a framework for The Five Keys for Hope** (which will be covered here in this chapter).

I invite you to investigate all of the programs that Kathryn and her team have created, to activate hope around the world including Hopeful Cities© which is equipping cities around the world with the tools they need to create, maintain, and grow hope, citywide. To activate hope in your community see the free Hopeful Cities Playbook at www.hopefulcities.org.

You also might want to check out Kathryn's book The **Biggest Little Book About Hope**, and her podcast **The Hope Matrix podcast**.

And, let's all mark on our calendars the **International Day of Hope**, celebrating the Science of Hope on the **first Monday in May**, to help normalize hopelessness, and share skills to activate hope. www.international-dayofhope.org

Why Hope?

(From www.hopefulminds.org)

Hope is critical to all aspects of life. Hope science shows higher hope equates to better grades, economic success, improved health and well-being, longer life, less violence, more resilience, increased confidence, improved leadership, better employee engagement, and more. The Hopeful Minds program was created to test the hypothesis that ***hope is teachable,*** and the research confirms it to be true.

Hopelessness is the single consistent predictor of suicide, the primary symptom of depression, and a predictor of weapon carrying on school property, violence, self-harm, substance misuse, and more. It consists of both emotional despair and motivational helplessness, and what we consider the opposite of hope is prevalent among youth and can permeate into adulthood.

Hopelessness is the leading predictor of suicide and the number one symptom of depression. **Higher hope**, on the other hand, corresponds to greater academic achievement, improved health, increased productivity, less anxiety and depression, less violence, more social support and connection, and less loneliness. Our focus is on the prevention of anxiety and depression, through teaching life skills for creating, maintaining, and sustaining Hope with practical tools and exercises.

What is HOPE?

(excerpted from Hopeful Minds Lesson One)

Merriam-Webster's Dictionary defines hope as the feeling of wanting something to happen and thinking that it can happen. We disagree with this definition, as it leaves out the important 'action' aspect of hope. Webster's definition more accurately reflects that of a 'wish.' Hope and wish are often used interchangeably in the media, which negatively impacts the global understanding of the need for hope. It's time to redefine our understanding of hope because science has taught us one thing for sure; a hope is not a wish. **A hope is a vision for something in the future, fueled by both positive feelings and inspired actions.**

Positive feelings are those feelings that help us to stay hopeful as we work towards our goals.

Inspired or smart actions are actions that propel us toward our goals.

Hope is a skill that every single one of us must learn, as it influences all the areas of our lives. By choosing hope you are choosing to make a lasting, positive impact on your future.

The Science of Hope

From www.hopefulmindsets.com

The Science of Hope is based on years of research that shows hope predicts academic success above IQ, athletic performance beyond ability, recovery time from disease, safety in the workplace, connection with others, graduation likelihood from school, engagement on the job, and more. Hope is a known **protective** factor for anxiety, depression, addiction, and suicide.

You can actually measure how hopeful you are, and work to improve your hope (see Hope Score at www.hopefulmindsets.com). Hope is not fixed, and you can learn it at any age. You need to practice skills to improve your hope, which is where the SHINE framework comes in handy.

Hopeful Mindsets™ is based on the work of leading experts on Hope, Mindset, Mental Health, Stress, Positive Psychology, Business, Communications, and more. Using the **Five Keys to SHINE Hope™** as a foundation, Hopeful Mindsets takes them a step further, suggesting that using these Five Keys and applying them to any situation can take you from hopelessness, to hope.

Hope is an innovative way to address mental health, as it is **preventative** in nature. Just because you have experienced anxiety and depression doesn't mean it is your destiny, as you can proactively practice and manage your hope. So while this process doesn't *treat* depression or anxiety, it *does teach* the "how-to" of hope.

This work started based on Lin Abramson's definition of hopelessness that hopelessness is both emotional (despair) and motivational (helplessness). That is why learning hope emphasizes how to get out of despair to positive feelings, and from helplessness to inspired action.

The Five Keys to
SHINE Hope™

STRESS SKILLS 

HAPPINESS HABITS 

INSPIRED ACTIONS 

NOURISHING NETWORK 

ELIMINATE CHALLENGES

© 2021, Innovative Analysis, LLC.

THE FIVE KEYS TO SHINE HOPE™

I encourage you to get familiar with and start being proactive about maintaining a sense of hope no matter how many challenges are ahead.

Here you'll find outlined skills associated with each key so that you can start practicing them.

Each of these keys for hope will help you create, maintain, and grow your hope.

- **Stress Skills**
- **Happiness Habits**
- **Inspired Actions**
- **Nourishing Network**
- **Eliminate Challenges**

S TRESS SKILLS

Stress Skills are actions that help you navigate your stress response and work through your body's chemical response to external stimuli. By practicing them, you are teaching yourself how to proactively manage the *emotional despair* found in hopelessness and move towards positive feelings where you activate hope.

The Stress Response

This is when you are emotionally triggered by something in your environment, and you go into fight, flight, freeze, or fawn mode as your body releases stress hormones, such as cortisol, adrenaline, and norepinephrine. You are in your downstairs brain, and can't reach your upstairs brain; the upstairs brain is the place where you make good decisions for moving towards all you hope for in life.

Stress Skills

90 Second Pause
Deep Belly Breathing
Napping
Calming Music
Reaffirming beliefs
Visualization
Sensory
Engagement
Punching a Pillow

Crying
Prayer
Walk in Nature
Meditation
Yoga
Decluttering

Focus on strengths
Journaling
Exercise
Gardening
Time Near Water
and Nature

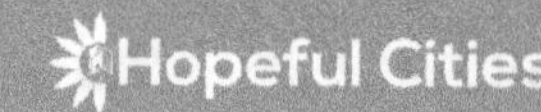

Hopeful Cities

Join the Global Hopeful Cities Movement
at **www.hopefulcities.org**

© 2021 Innovative Analysis, LLC

Key 1: Stress Skills

When you are emotionally triggered by something in your environment, you go into fight, flight, freeze, or fawn mode as your body releases stress hormones. This is called your stress response.

Stress Skills are skills that help you navigate your stress response, calm yourself down, and return to a hopeful mindset. By practicing Stress Skills, you are teaching yourself how to work through your body's chemical response to external stimuli and then respond calmly.

Try these Stress Skills for Serenity

- **90-Second Pause**
- **Meditation** *(see Chapter 7)*
- **Breathing Techniques**
- **Sleep**
- **Calming Music**
- **Visualization**
- **Time near water and nature**
- **Journaling**
- **Exercise**
- **Engaging Senses**
- **Gardening**
- **Massage**
- **Tapping**
- **Laughter**
- **Yoga**

Ⓗ APPINESS HABITS

Happiness Habits are healthy, long-term actions that cause your brain to release happiness hormones including endorphins, dopamine, serotonin, and oxytocin. Happiness Habits help you stay in your upstairs brain, where you access the problem-solving skills, collaboration, and passion critical for hope.

Positive Feelings

Positive feelings, the first ingredient of hope, are feelings that are located in your upstairs brain like wonder, joy, and peace that make it easier to overcome obstacles that get in the way of hope. You proactively manage the emotional despair of hopelessness using Stress Skills and use your Happiness Habits to stay in your upstairs brain, where you then energetically move towards your goals in life.

Happiness Habits

Utilizing strengths	Showing Gratitude and Kindness	Sleeping
Pursuing passion	Playing Games	Nutrition
Activating purpose	Volunteering	Dancing and Singing
Smiling	Time with Family and Friends	Donating
Exercising	Experiencing Wonder & Awe	Giving a hug
Playing or Listening to Music	Practicing Faith	Setting Goals
Spending time in Nature		Practicing Affirmations

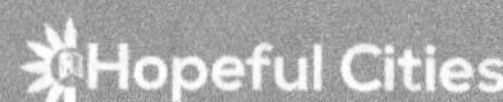

Join the Global Hopeful Cities Movement at www.hopefulcities.org

© 2021 Innovative Analysis, LLC

Key 2: Happiness Habits

Positive feelings, the first ingredient of hope, are feelings that are located in your upstairs brain. They are the feelings that help you maintain a hopeful mindset and encourage you to keep moving toward your goals. So, if you want to have a strong hopeful mindset, you want to spend as much time as possible in your upstairs brain.

The Upstairs Brain, or the prefrontal cortex, is where thinking, imagining, and learning occur. This part of the brain is responsible for the development of sound decision-making and planning, control over emotions and body, and self-understanding and empathy. The upstairs brain is also where we access our positive feelings.

Happiness Habits for Positivity

Happiness Habits are healthy, long-term actions that you can take to foster positive feelings and stay in your upstairs brain.

- **A Morning Routine**
- **Smiling**
- **Exercise**
- **Uplifting Music**

- **Nature**
- **Playing an Instrument**
- **Singing**
- **Gratitude**
- **Kindness**
- **Games**
- **Volunteering**
- **Family**
- **Friends**
- **Wonder**
- **Awe**
- **Faith**
- **Pursuing Passions**
- **Fulfilling Purposes**
- **Learning New Things**
- **Volunteer Work**
- **Saving Money**
- **Affirmation**
- **Laughter**
- **Nutrition**

INSPIRED ACTIONS

Inspired Actions, the second ingredient of hope, are the deliberate steps you take toward your goals in life. Inspired Actions help you to move away from the motivational helplessness, the second ingredient of hopelessness, and toward what you are hopeful for in life.

Types of Goals:

- ✓ WOOP
- ✓ Achievement
- ✓ Intrinsic
- ✓ SMART
- ✓ Stretch
- ✓ Micro-Goals

Pathways, Agency, and Regoaling

Obstacles are inevitable, and sometimes you can't reach the goal as you intended. It is important to embrace obstacles to goals, learn to pivot or reevaluate, be flexible and adaptable, and never be afraid to ask for help.

If a goal seems too big, use the stepping process or create micro-goals to chunk it down into smaller goals. Think of one thing you can do in the next 20 minutes. And know when you need to re-goal.

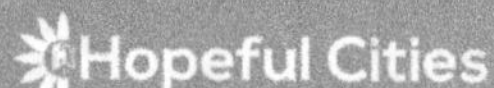

Key 3: Inspired Actions

Inspired actions are the second ingredient of hope.

You can practice inspired actions by creating purposeful goals. You can use:

1. **Stretch Goals**
2. **Achievement Goals**
3. **SMART Goals**

Purposeful goals help you keep a hopeful mindset by giving you something to look forward to and encouraging you to work towards your future.

Remember:

- Your goals should always be SMART: Specific, Measurable, Attainable, Relevant, and Time-bound
- If your goal seems too big, chunk it down into smaller goals (also known as stepping).
- Obstacles are a part of life. Embrace the obstacle and learn to pivot, reevaluate, re-goal, and ask for help.

NOURISHING NETWORKS

Your Nourishing Networks, also known as your Hope Networks, are the people in your life that provide you with support, help you stay on track, encourage you to succeed, and who you do the same for in return. You are up to 95% more likely to achieve a goal if you write it down, and check in with someone regularly. So Nourishing Networks are critical support systems for moving you towards what you hope for in life.

Your Hope Networks should include:

- ✓ People who know and understand you.
- ✓ People who value your strengths.
- ✓ People who activate the SHINE framework.
- ✓ People whom you trust and can confide in.
- ✓ People who are available to support you.
- ✓ People you are willing to do the above for as well.

Enhancing Your Hope Networks

Enhance your Hope Networks using the 5:1 rule, vulnerability, praise, recognition, kindness, gratitude, empathy, compassion, collaboration, and strong communication, and be sure to have different networks for different areas of life.

Don't forget to include doctors, therapists, and/or other medical professionals in your Hope Networks.

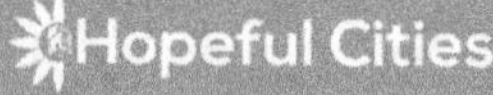

Key 4: Nourishing Networks

Choose your family, friends, or coworkers who can provide support, and help you stay on track. Make sure they see the best in you and want you to succeed. Also, be sure to include doctors, therapists, psychologists, faith leaders, and/or other medical professionals.

Make sure you know where to go in times of crisis, when the people around you may not be able to provide the support you need.

Your Hope Network should only include:

- People who know and understand you
- People who value your strengths
- People who contribute to your hopeful mindset
- People in whom you can confide
- People who are available to support you

Enhance Your Hope Network with:

- 5:1 Rule
- Vulnerability
- Recognition
- Kindness
- Empathy
- Strong Communication

ELIMINATING CHALLENGES

Challenges to Hope are negative habits of thought that quickly take you to hopelessness, that emotional despair and sense of helplessness. The thought patterns are often unconscious habits, so becoming aware of these patterns is critical. Once we know what they are and recognize them, it is important to counteract them so that we don't let them keep us from all we hope for in life.

Eliminating Challenges

Most of the Challenges to Hope take constant, repetitive actions to change and overcome. Thanks to the science of neuroplasticity, we know it is possible with practice and dedication. The key is to learn to identify what specific challenges happen most frequently and then proactively find ways to manage those challenges.

Challenges to Hope

Limiting Beliefs
Automatic Negative Thoughts (ANTs)
All-or-Nothing Thinking
Negative Bias

Rumination
Worry
Focusing on the Uncontrollable
Attaching to Outcomes
Internalizing Failure

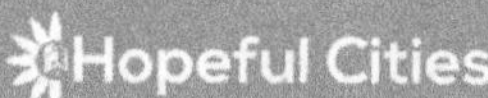

Join the Global Hopeful Cities Movement at **www.hopefulcities.org**

© 2021 Innovative Analysis LLC

Key 5: Eliminate Challenges

Most of the Challenges to Hope are habits of thought and take constant, repetitive actions to change them. Thanks to the science of neuroplasticity, we know it is possible with practice and dedication. Challenges to Hope can quickly take you from hope to hopelessness. However, once you identify these Challenges to Hope, you can use your Stress Skills, Happiness Habits, Inspired Actions, and Hope Network to overcome them.

Challenges to Hope:

- **Rumination**
- **Worry**
- **Internalizing Failure**
- **Focusing on the Uncontrollable**
- **Automatic Negative Thoughts**
- **Limiting Beliefs**

More resources for Learning Hope

If you are in crisis, text HOME to 741741 to connect with a crisis counselor.

Want to learn more about how to create, sustain, and grow Hopeful Mindsets?

Join the Hopeful Mindsets Movement at: **hopefulmind sets.com** *© 2021, Innovative Analysis, LLC.*

10% of the proceeds from this book are being donated to iFred.org to help continue their work with destigmatizing depression and teaching Hope.

Key takeaway:

When all else seems overwhelming, hope is a powerful force that can keep us going. It is a teachable skill. It is measurable. So no matter what you're going through, with hope, you will have the power to move through it.

6

CALMING THE STORM

The secret of your future is hidden in your daily routine.

— MIKE MURDOCK

CREATING STRUCTURE IN YOUR LIFE

The symptoms of bipolar disorder often cause a sense of instability in a person's life. Due to frequent mood shifts and unpredictable behaviors, some aspects of daily life can feel uncertain or unreliable. To combat this instability and get more control over your life, you must structure your days to suit your needs.

As mentioned in chapter three, you can create structure in your life by establishing healthy habits, routines, and rituals that boost your mood and make you feel safe. Implementing a schedule of specific exercises and activities will benefit your mind and body. Don't worry if you are someone who finds it difficult to stick to strict routines. Your schedule can be as flexible or as rigid as you choose, as long as it involves doing things that make you feel calm and stable.

Having a daily routine can also build your confidence and self-reliance. If you consider yourself to be an independent person who thrives on taking care of yourself, you may find routines to be an easy confidence booster. For people who have low self-esteem, or are going through depression, it can feel impossible to help yourself. Your negative thought processes can prevent you from seeing how capable you really are. Establishing realistic daily routines or rituals that you are able to complete can build your self-esteem back up, as well as remind you that you can rely on your abilities.

Develop Schedules and Routines

There are several ways to develop a schedule or routine that you benefit from. You can work with a therapist to determine what activities or habits will have a positive impact on your daily life. You can also take inspiration from other people's routines that impress or motivate you. Your routine is for you and you only. You should not worry too much about making it unique, exciting, or trendy. As long as you feel productive and successful while completing your tasks, it is the perfect routine for you.

Developing a routine also does not mean you have to rely on specific start and end times. For the most part, your routine should happen in the same order every day to encourage consistency and habit-building. However, you do not have to be so strict with yourself that you feel ashamed or guilty if you alter a step when needed. Routines help you find a daily rhythm that is simple to remember and follow. They can also give you a feeling of familiarity when life feels overwhelming or daunting. On top of these benefits, having a healthy routine may limit any impulsive behaviors that can cause harm to your well-being.

To start creating a routine, use a calendar or blank sheet of paper to visualize your schedule. You may even have the ability to use your phone or computer, depending on your comfort with technology. Begin by deciding the length of time over which your routine will take place: a day, week, or even hourly. If you are just starting out, it will probably be easiest to start with a day or week.

Using your calendar or a blank sheet of paper, fill in every appointment or event that you already have scheduled, plus their starting times. These can be doctor appointments, therapy sessions, meetings with friends, or anything in between. Once you have these written down, you will be better able to visualize your free time.

Next, decide which activities are a "must-do." Brushing your teeth, making your bed, taking your medications or vitamins, and eating a nutritious meal are some examples. You may already have an idea of what tasks are most important for your mental health. If so, add them to a list with your other "must-do's." Choose when these tasks should be completed throughout your day, in between other scheduled events. Add the general starting time of when these tasks will occur.

When you have your "must-do's" added to your calendar or paper, choose one or two self-care activities to add to your routine. Self-care looks different for everybody. Some people prefer to take a walk in nature, while others like a warm bubble bath. Decide which self-care activities matter most to you and make you feel the best. Then, you can add them to your schedule at times you feel are fitting.

According to a 2020 article published on VeryWell Mind, your routine should not stop there. In addition to "must-do's" and self-care tasks, you should add one task for each of the following intentions: a task that connects you with other people, like friends or family; a task that is meaningful to you, like helping others or volunteering your time; and a task that feels productive, like paying your bills or cleaning your home (Salters-Pedneault, 2020). You do not need to overwhelm your schedule with hefty tasks in these areas. Choose ones that feel realistic and manageable alongside the rest of your routine.

Once you have filled your schedule with a good routine, it's time to test it out! Follow your routine exactly as you've written it and see how it makes you feel. If it seems like a good fit for your abilities and schedule, repeat the routine every day. Do this as consistently as possible in order to make it feel like a natural progression of your time.

It may help you to keep a visual of your routine in a place you will look at every day. A calendar, list of tasks, or sticky note reminding you of your intentions can motivate you on days when you feel less inclined to follow your routine. Many people also find it beneficial to eliminate tasks as they are completed, either by crossing them off or erasing them from the schedule. This can give you a feeling of productivity and motivate you to move on to the next step of your routine. Keep in mind that your routine does not have to be filled with big activities or accomplishments. Something as minor as making your bed in the morning can give you enough momentum to move forward.

Example of a Healthy Routine

If you need some guidance on creating a good routine for yourself, take a look at the example below. It can provide you with ideas and inspiration that you may not have considered otherwise.

Weekday Routine:

- Wake up and do daily spiritual practice
- Eat a healthy breakfast
- Brush my teeth
- Take medications and/or vitamins
- Put on an outfit that feels comfortable and brings me joy
- Go to work
- Connect with co-workers

- Eat a healthy lunch
- After work, take a 15-30 minute walk outside
- Help my elderly neighbor bring in her groceries
- Call a friend
- Eat a healthy dinner
- Put on cozy pajamas
- Reward myself with an episode of my favorite show
- Write down what I'm grateful for today
- Get a good night's sleep

Of course, this routine is just an example and does not have to be followed exactly, or at all. It simply serves as inspiration for your own routine. If any of the afore-mentioned tasks appeal to you, try them in your own routine. If they seem unrealistic or unappealing, ask yourself what sounds better. What matters most is that you identify activities that bring you happiness, peace, and satisfaction.

Set Up Helpful Habits

Habitual behaviors are ingrained in routines. One component of a successful, healthy routine is to break any bad habits you may have. These types of habits can be negative self-talk, indulging in dangerous or unhealthy behaviors, or even spending time with people who bring you down. When you do these things often enough, you begin to depend on them for stability, instead of depending on habits that benefit you. For instance, if you are used to hanging out with someone who degrades or talks down to you, you may begin to agree with them. Allowing yourself to be in such a negative presence will only hurt your mindset and cause you to treat yourself poorly. Breaking this habit by spending less time with such a negative person and more time with someone who is positive can help you reframe your perspective of yourself.

Breaking bad habits is not as easy as it may seem. Because these behaviors are so intertwined with your daily life, it can take a long time to stop acting on them. Statistically speaking, it can take around 66 days to change a habit (Krause, 2016). Depending on how your mind and body work, it can be a shorter or longer period. The key to changing your habits is to take your time and try not to rush to get the result. Remember, you're retraining your brain to do something new. It will be more effective for you to go slow and steady during the process.

To form healthy, helpful habits for your daily routine, start small. You do not need to overload your brain with multiple habit changes, no matter how much you want to improve your lifestyle. Beginning the process with one desired habit change will give you a good basis on which to build more habits. On top of that, it may be easier for you to replace your bad habits with healthier ones, rather than trying to stop the negative behaviors altogether.

For example, if you know that binge-watching television shows makes your depressive symptoms worse, try to replace that habit with one that takes you away from the screen. Instead of sitting down and watching hours of your favorite show, causing you to disconnect from the world and avoid your feelings, you can sit down with an interesting book or creative activity. Start by replacing one hour of television time with one hour of reading or doing something that engages your imagination. Over time, your mind and body will find the same peace in these activities as it did with mindlessly watching television.

If you have a routine that works for you, aside from a bad habit or two, add a replacement habit to the schedule. It can be something as small as drinking a glass of water after eating breakfast, or something as big as going for a 30-minute walk after work or class. Make your habit a consistent part of the routine you have already developed and it will soon feel like you have been doing it all along.

Sometimes, you will forget or choose to skip a day of building your habit, and that's okay. Everybody needs a break every once in a while—you should not give up on your efforts if it happens to you. If you miss a day or indulge in the bad habit you are trying to replace, remind yourself of your intentions to be healthier and happier; you can always try again the next day. If you continuously choose to ignore the new habit, you may need to re-evaluate if it is a habit that feels right for your routine.

Don't forget to reward yourself! When you remember to perform your new habit, treat yourself to something that makes you happy. A powerful reward system, like your favorite activity or snack, will train your brain to perform your new habit more consistently in order to receive the reward.

You will know when your attempt at building a new habit is successful when it becomes something you do without thinking. Once you notice that a habit you have been trying to form has become so ingrained in your routine that it feels natural, you can bask in your success. You may even feel uncomfortable at the idea of *not* doing the habit because it has become such a consistent part of your schedule. When you reach this point, celebrate your victory and see what else you can turn into a healthy habit!

Habit Planning Activity

For guidance on establishing healthy habits, consider using a habit planner. A habit planner can be used to list out desired habits and keep track of intentions. To make your own, write down which negative habit you would like to replace and why. Then, write down the healthy habit you will use to replace it, followed by how it will make a positive impact.

Afterward, write down your intention with building this new habit. Why is it important to you to change? What outcome are you hoping for or expecting when this habit is replaced? Being able to understand why you want to form a new habit will give you more motivation to act, as it shows how it will help you in the future.

When you've listed your habits and intentions, make a note of how you will reward yourself when you remember to work on building the new habit. Feel free to make this part as colorful or noticeable as you want, as it will serve as motivation for you. The more exciting the reward seems, the more likely you are to work toward achieving it.

Therapist Aid is a website that provides various worksheets, guides, and interactive tools relating to mental and emotional wellness. The organization has published a Habit Plan worksheet to allow users to visualize how they will build new habits. The Therapist Aid Habit Plan is a simple but effective tool if you are interested in developing healthy habits to manage your bipolar disorder. Below you can find a link to download the free PDF worksheet on TherapistAid.com:

https://www.therapistaid.com/therapy-worksheet/habit-plan#

Key Takeaway:

A proven method for encouraging emotional wellness is to create structure in your life. Bipolar disorder can cause you to feel unstable and unpredictable, especially regarding your moods and behaviors. Living with routines can transform your daily life from one that is emotionally and physically taxing to one that makes you feel happy and satisfied.

It will benefit you greatly to establish a daily routine that involves social connection, self-care, productivity, and healthy habits. When you implement such structure into your life, you will begin to feel more centered and at peace.

SOUL HEALING–DAILY MEDITATIONS

"*In the midst of movement and chaos, keep stillness inside of you.*"

— ANONYMOUS

Meditation can give you a sense of calm, peace, and balance that can benefit both your emotional well-being and your overall health. You can also use it to relax and cope with stress by refocusing your attention on something calming. Meditation can help you learn to stay centered and keep inner peace.

Studies show that mediation helps in quantifiable ways. Of the people surveyed:

- Improve concentration and memory (53%)
- Better performance at work and/or school (52%)
- Increase energy (39%)
- General health and wellness (30%)
- Improved attitude and outlook on life (28%)

(https://mellowed.com/meditation-statistics/)

Developing a daily practice is something that I (and many others) recommend that EVERYONE does. The "practice" can be a variety of things, with the common denominator of helping you be in the present moment, get centered, and connect to whatever is your higher power/life force. For some, taking a walk in nature is their daily practice, others prefer doing meditations, and others read a daily message and then pray or meditate on it. The time limit can be whatever you want.

The choices are endless. The most important thing is doing it consistently. Shoot for at least 5 out of 7 days a week.

Over the years I've tried out many different things including listening to a soulful song, reading a passage in a book I liked, listening to guided meditations, connecting to my higher power, listing things I'm grateful for...and more. I seem to stick with one thing for several weeks, then it morphs into something else. And that's OK! The main thing is that I'm doing SOMETHING almost every day that helps me to just BE and BE PRESENT for a few minutes. My practice varies from 10-20 minutes, and I do mine first thing before I even get out of bed. (Otherwise, the activities of my day take over and it's hard for me to stop and focus on my practice.)

If you don't already have a daily practice, you might want to use the meditations I've included here to get you started. Try it first thing in the morning, or perhaps before going to bed. At first, it may seem a bit forced – but that's just because you are developing a new habit. I encourage you to stick with it though. If you miss a day, it's OK. Pick it back up the next day. I found that the more I did my daily practice, the more I loved it, and now I find it hard to start my day without it!

Another easy way to get started is to download a meditation app or just go to YouTube. These are great free or low-cost resources. I've listed a few below that you might want to try out.

Find with works for you and do your best to do it consistently. A daily practice has the potential to bring moments of peace, calm, and joy into your life.

Meditations For You

The meditations/breathing exercises I have provided for you in the chapter are suitable for anyone. I hope that they will provide opportunities for you to become present in the moment, release your thoughts, worries, and stress, and find a sense of inner peace. There is no right or wrong way to do them. I suggest either sitting or lying down in a place where you won't have any distractions. I've included a variety of lengths so you can find the ones that resonate the most with you.

For the print version, please read the meditations slowly to yourself, stopping as needed to take in what you just read. On the audio version, listen and take in the words that you are hearing.

The meditations included in this book are:

- **Box Breathing**, an Ayurvedic form of breathwork called pranayama that originated in India *(Sanskrit word, Ayurveda, translates to knowledge of life.)*
- **Short Guided Visualization for Centering**, original meditation by C.A. Cook
- **Allowing Joy, Safe Space** and **You Are Worthy Meditations**, used with permission from *Guided Meditations for Anxiety, Trauma, Addiction and Self-Healing* Book by The Mindfulness Mentors
- **Positive Attitude Meditation**, used with permission from Merilu Hill

Other great resources for Affirmations and Meditations on YouTube are:

- Abraham Hicks Official YouTube Channel: www.youtube.com/@AbrahamHicks
- Louise Hay Official YouTube Channel: www.youtube.com/@louisehay9748
- Meditation and Healing Channel: www.youtube.com/@MeditationandHealing
- Meditation for Manic and Bipolar Episodes: www.youtube.com/watch?v=nsPso6VxZ2I

- Music Therapy for Bipolar Disorder Manic Depression: www.youtube.com/watch?v=0E53ZZa3Qk8
- 10-Minute Meditation For Depression: www.youtube.com/watch?v=xRxT9cOKiM8
- Tapping Meditation for Release Stress, Anxiety & Overwhelm (from the Tapping Solution): www.youtube.com/watch?v=Sqe3h3l8a7w

BOX BREATHING

Let's start with the simplest of "meditations" which is really a breathing technique. Box Breathing is rooted in an Ayurvedic form of breathwork called pranayama that originated in India and is practiced in yoga, explains Tal Rabinowitz, founder, and CEO of The DEN Meditation in Los Angeles. "It has incredibly ancient roots, with different techniques for calming, bringing in energy, refining focus, and relaxing the nervous system; however, the military popularized it and brought it mainstream," she says. "Mark Divine, a former Navy SEAL who is also a very experienced martial artist, introduced it to the special operations community in the military, showing the world that by simply breathing, you can achieve the desired calming effects in just moments."

I begin almost every workshop or presentation I give with Box Breathing. It's very easy to do and can be done anywhere. (Next time you are in a long line and start feeling agitated just try doing some Box Breathing and see how much it helps to calm you down.)

You will be inhaling to a count of 4, holding for a count of 4, exhaling for a count of 4, and holding for a count of 4. If you want, you can imagine drawing a box in your head while you are breathing to help you follow along (like in this diagram).

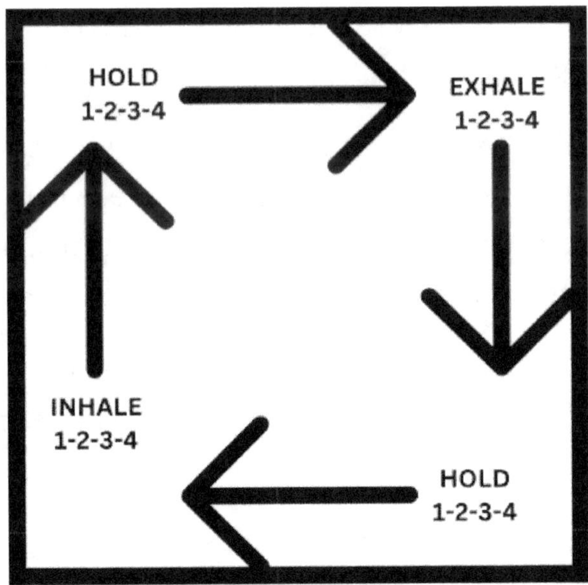

You can do 3 – 5 rounds or set a timer for 3 – 5 minutes and do as many as you can in that timeframe.

- Inhale: 1, 2, 3, 4
- Hold: 1, 2, 3, 4
- Exhale: 1, 2, 3, 4
- Hold: 1, 2, 3, 4
- **Repeat this breathing sequence.**

AHHHHHH…doesn't doing that short breathing technique help to calm down your nervous system and ground you into this present moment? I hope so! (And if it didn't, I encourage you to do it again.)

SHORT GUIDED VISUALIZATION FOR CENTERING

I originally wrote this meditation for my Vision Board workshops, but it can be used at any time to help you to get centered and to remind yourself of the magnificent being that you are.

To do this I will give you prompts to ponder. Then you can read the next one, ponder it, the next one, ponder it, etc.

To start, I'd like for you to close your eyes and take 3 deep breaths, bringing your mind, body, and soul into this present moment.

When you feel like you are in this space, open your eyes and read the next prompt.

Close your eyes again and connect yourself to whatever is your higher power/life source. Bring your attention to your heart and bring to mind several things you are grateful for.

When you are complete with that, open your eyes and read the next prompt.

Close your eyes again, bringing your attention back to your heart. Imagine a flame burning and as you watch it, it grows bigger and brighter. This flame represents your unique dreams that you hold in your heart.

When you are complete with that, open your eyes and read the next prompt.

Close your eyes again and go back to that flame, burning bright in your heart. Visualize beams of light shooting out from this light into the world. This represents you sharing your unique dreams with the world. Then see that light touching hundreds (maybe thousands) of people and animals.

Hold that vision in your mind for a minute or two, then open your eyes and read the next prompt.

Close your eyes and go back to that flame that is beaming out into the world, touching SOOO many people and animals. Now see them THANKING YOU

for sharing your unique dreams and light with them. Really take in the gratitude they are giving back to you in this moment.

Hold that vision in your mind for a minute or two.

When you are complete with that, take 3 deep breaths and open your eyes when you are ready.

I hope that this visualization allows you to see that YOUR UNIQUE DREAMS and YOUR LIGHT MATTER!!

The following Meditations are being used with permission from the book **"Guided Meditations for Anxiety, Trauma, Addiction, and Self-Healing"**by The Mindfulness Mentors.

It is available on Kindle and Audible at: https://amzn.to/3YwZmfF

ALLOWING JOY

Before beginning this meditation, please keep in mind:

- ➤ Why you chose this topic
- ➤ How do your belly, chest, and head each feel when you reflect on this topic
- ➤ The emotions that you can associate with these visceral feelings
- ➤ The positive or negative impact of any stories you believe in regarding this topic
- ➤ The fact that many others are feeling similarly about this topic as you
- ➤ How you might feel with increased awareness around this topic
- ➤ When you can apply increased mindfulness to this topic in your day-to-day life

Welcome to your practice
Find comfort and stillness
I invite you to be gently guided
Trace the path of your breath
As you breathe in through the nose
And exhale through the lips
Feel the breath on the inside of the nose
And on the back of the lungs as the breath pours into
the body
Feel the places where your sit bones meet the support
beneath you
Find softness in all of the muscles in the face neck
and jaw
Relax the muscles around the eyes and eyelids
Let the shoulders settle away from the ears
Remember the last time you felt joy
Take yourself to that moment
Immersing yourself in the small details of this memory
The sounds, feelings, and sensations
The people who were surrounding you
What about this moment inspired such joy
Remember the joy you felt as a child
Reconnect to the joy you felt for being alive
The excitement of playing in the rain
The awe at the sight of a rainbow
The way the summer air felt against your skin
The flicker of lightning bugs

Feeling safe, protected, loved, and secure allows us to
experience joy
What did you need as a child to feel loved and
protected and safe
What about now
What do you need to feel safe and secure
As we ground into security
We create space for joy
Was there a time or a moment when you stopped
believing that
you were worthy of a joyful life
When did you lose your joy
What would it look like if joy and bliss were your
compasses
What would your days look like if you followed
your joy
If you followed your joy when you started your day
In the way you move your body
In the places you go and the way in which you connect
with others
In the work that you do in this world
Can you connect to the joy of simply being alive
Life's simple pleasures that you enjoy most
The joy in seeing the colors of the sunset
The feeling of an evening breeze against your skin
The smell of pine trees in the forest
To ability experience the ocean

The embrace of a loved one
To savor a warm drink on a cold night
To love
To connect
To be
Allow this joy to expand
Begin to deepen your breath
Let images dissolve and fade
Finding comfort in the constant of the breath
Become aware of your surroundings
Slowly start to return
Invite gentle movement in the fingers and toes
As you move into your next moments give yourself
permission to follow joy in simple ways
Thank you for practicing with me today.

SAFE SPACE

Before beginning this meditation, please keep in mind:

➤ Why you chose this topic
➤ How do your belly, chest, and head each feel
when you reflect on this topic
➤ The emotions that you can associate with
these visceral feelings
➤ The positive or negative impact of any stories
you believe in regarding this topic

➤ The fact that many others are feeling similarly about this topic as you

➤ How you might feel with increased awareness around this topic

➤ When you can apply increased mindfulness to this topic in your day-to-day life

Welcome to your practice
This meditation will support you in feeling safe and restoring and calming the nervous system
If your mind wanders, you can notice its wandering without judgment
Your breath will be your anchor throughout your practice, a support where you can rest your focus at anytime
Find a comfortable seated position
Allow the body to anchor down into the support beneath you
Feel the weight of your body resting into this support
Take a deep breath in through the nose, hold it at the top, and exhale with a sigh
Find a natural paced breath, breathing fully and evenly
Perhaps inhaling and exhaling for 6 counts each
Softly close your eyes, drawing your attention and focus inward
Let your focus rest with the breath
Forming a connection between the mind with the body as the breath circulates

Feel the expansion as you inhale and the softness and
ease as you exhale
Notice the pace and nature of the breath, whether it
feels slow or fast, full or shallow
Imagine walking a pathway lined with trees
Perhaps deep in the forest, on a tropical island, or a
place you've imagined
Imagine how the air would feel against your skin
The smells of pine or salt in the air
The vibrant flowers and leaves that would surround
you
The sounds of birds in the trees overhead
This pathway leads you to a large doorway up ahead
With each step you take, invite the body to relax and to
soften
Perhaps silently repeating soften, soften with each exhale
On the other side of the door ahead lies your own
personal safe space
A haven all your own, filled with the colors, textures,
and surroundings that make you feel comforted
A place where you would feel safe to relax and safe to
be yourself
You could envision a place you've visited, a place you've
only seen in photos or your imagination, or even a
room in your own home
Envision approaching the doorway

Take a deep breath in through the nose and exhale with
a sigh
Imagine opening the doorway and stepping through
the threshold into your safe haven
Perhaps it is outdoors
Or inside
You could imagine a house on the beach
A room in your own home
A seat next to a stream in a forest
A sun-filled glade
Continue to breathe fully and evenly
As you do, immerse yourself in the colors, textures, and
sounds you would be met with
The surface against your feet
The smell of your favorite coffee brewing or tea
waiting for you
Perhaps the salty smell of the ocean breeze blows
through the window
Perhaps you see your favorite books in a nook
Or candles warming the space with flickering warm
flames
Your pet or furry friend waiting there for you
Blankets, and cushions, art supplies, or simply pristine
and serene nature
Take your time to explore this place that is designed
just for you

Begin to focus on a point in this space where you could
fully let go and relax the body
A sea of blankets and pillows
A cushion overlooking the ocean
Floating in the ocean or a bathtub
Resting in a field of grass
Feel the weight of your body against the support
beneath you
Allow your body to fully rest into the support that is all
around you
Let go of the need to control your body in any way
Softening around the eyelids, brow, and cheeks
Unclenching the jaw and softening the lips
Melting the shoulders away from the spine
Take three deep breaths in through the nose and out
with a sigh
In the stillness and the silence notice what is here for you
Notice the emotions that are being expressed through
physical sensations in the body
The pain expressed as tension
The fear expressed in tightness of the throat
Anger as a warming or heat rising in the chest
Release these physical sensations to give way to the
emotions beneath
Allowing the emotion or emotions to unravel without
force

Can you hold these emotions without judgment or expectation

What does this part of you need to feel supported, nurtured and safe

Listen to the thoughts that arise with curiosity and open observation

What does the mind need to feel supported

What does the body need to feel supported

Connect to your inner voice

The voice reminding you of your needs, desires, preferences, and values

The subtle nudges and inspirations that arise in stillness and silence

Perhaps nudging you to take an opportunity, set a boundary

An indication of support you need in some way

Nudges to pursue a passion, to care for yourself, or to receive support in some way

In the stillness and silence, notice the awareness that is always present, always a part of you

The part of you that watches and observes your experience

A reminder that deep down, you are conscious awareness

When you feel a sense of completion, draw your focus back to your safe space

Once more sinking into the colors, the textures, sounds
and smells
All of the unique flavors of this space
Know that this space is always available for you to
return whenever you like
For the next three rounds of breath, I invite you to take
two inhales followed by a long exhale
It may sound like:
Inhale……….. Inhale……….
long exhale…………………
Inhale………. Inhale……….
long exhale…………………
Inhale………. Inhale……….
long exhale…………………
When you are ready, imagine walking out of the door
of this space
Allow the images to dissolve and fade
Returning your focus once again to the breath
Notice if the body feels relaxed, heavy, tired, energized
Begin to take a deeper, more audible breath
Roll the shoulders up and away from the ears
Bring the hands together, rubbing them together to
create heat and friction and gently massaging your
hands into your neck or shoulders
As you're ready, open your eyes and lift your gaze,
returning to the room and giving yourself plenty of
time to gently transition back to your day

Thank you for practicing with me, I look forward to connecting with you soon.

YOU ARE WORTHY

Before beginning this meditation, please keep in mind:

➤ Why you chose this topic
➤ How do your belly, chest, and head each feel when you reflect on this topic
➤ The emotions that you can associate with these visceral feelings
➤ The positive or negative impact of any stories you believe in regarding this topic
➤ The fact that many others are feeling similarly about this topic as you
➤ How you might feel with increased awareness around this topic
➤ When you can apply increased mindfulness to this topic in your day-to-day life

Welcome to your practice
Softly close your eyes
Feel the subtle energy in the space around you soft noises and hums
Notice if the air around you feels warm or cool against your skin

Breathe deeply
Exhale fully
Breathe deeply
Exhale fully
Breathing in through the nose expanding the belly
And releasing the air from the lungs completely as you
exhale
Feel the rise and fall of the abdomen
Soften the brows and eyelids
Soften the lips and jaw
Surrender into the support around you
Let your body land
Picture yourself as a baby
Perhaps imagining a photo that comes to mind
Knowing that this version of you
Was worthy of care, affection safety, connection,
and love
There was nothing you had to do to deserve this love
and care
You were worthy just because you are
Picture a version of you a bit older
As a child acknowledging that this version of you
Was just as worthy of love, attention, care, happiness,
and joy
This version of you was worthy of a beautiful life
When did you learn to forget your worth?
When did you first feel unworthy?

Your worth and value are infinite
You are just as worthy today as the day you were born
And every day in between
Your worth and potential have never changed or
diminished
Your value is constant, infinite, and eternal
Your worth is infinite and eternal
Your thoughts, feelings needs and ideas matter
Your life is of infinite worth
You are just as worthy as anyone and everyone else who
has ever lived
The same way you would greet that child version of
yourself with love and acceptance
Greet yourself with love
Just as you are in this moment
You are worthy of a beautiful life just because you exist
You are worthy of love, connection, attention, affection,
joy, and care in this moment
There is nothing you have to do to achieve worthiness
Who you are is worthy
There is nothing you need to fix about yourself
Think of how you believe and know the worthiness of
your best friend or a beloved family member
Can you imagine seeing yourself with the eyes of worth
Imagine pulling out a piece of paper and on that paper
writing the reasons you are worthy
I am worthy because I am alive

I am worthy because everyone is worthy of happiness
and love
I am worthy because I exist
And now write what you are worthy of
I am worthy of love and affection
I am worthy of peace
I am worthy of overflow
I am worthy of joy
I am worthy of respect and presence
Imagine resting that paper in the sea
And letting it float away
If you fully believed in your worthiness how would you
be speaking, thinking, and being
How would you care for yourself?
If you lived your life as if you were fully worthy
Imagine the small details
Imagine your day to day experience living each
moment as someone who loves themselves
This does not mean being perfect or acting correctly
But honoring how you feel and what you need in each
moment
Let those images dissolve and fade
Return to the awareness of your environment
Let the sounds and energy surround you
Feel the places where the air meets your skin
It's time to return
Slowly open your eyes and lift your gaze

I invite you to carry the energy you've cultivated today into your next moments
Be well.

The following Meditation is being used with permission from Merilu Hill - podcaster, educator, and author. You can learn more about her at: https://meriluhill.com.

POSITIVE ATTITUDE MEDITATION

When we develop that positive attitude, it's possible to start feeling better about yourself - you treat yourself with more respect...you love yourself...you have a stronger immune system...you can be more focused... and you're actually training your mind to be more positive.

One of the things that I really learned about meditation is my brain doesn't stop wandering. It wanders all the time. But as I listened to the meditations and take in my breath, I do I come back and bring my brain back and focus. So don't beat yourself up. When your mind wanders, just allow it to wander, and then come back.

Find yourself in a seated comfortable position or laying down. You can sit on the floor or on a chair. Just be sure that you sit in a way that your spine can be long and upright. Try to eliminate any disruptions or distractions for the duration of this meditation.

Let's begin.
Simply bring your awareness to your breath.
Breathe in and breathe out.
If you find your mind wandering, it's okay. Just gently bring it back. Don't beat yourself up. Just bring it back to the present.

Take time to feel yourself in the space.

Breathe in and breathe out.

I feel good about myself.

It's okay to like myself.

I am likeable.

I will not allow anxious thoughts to steal my joy.

Again, if you find your mind wandering, just gently bring it back.

Breathe in and breathe out.

I have many good qualities.

I choose to take good care of myself.

I may do some things wrong, but I'm doing many things right.

I learned from my mistakes and forgive myself when I make them.

Shame, blame, guilt, regret or anger have no power over me.

I evict shame, blame, guilt, regret and anger.

I may be one in 7 billion, but I'm also ONE in 7 billion.

I believe I can change the world.

I declare what I need and I give myself what I need.

I have everything I need to live a joyful and abundant life within me.

My life has a purpose.

I choose to see the good in people that I interact with today.

I have more compassion for myself and forgiveness for myself.

I love myself.

I love every part of me.

I love that I don't have to think about breathing.

Take a deep breath in and say "I am enough."

I've always been enough. Breathe out.

I can change the way I view my past.

Every experience that I've ever had made me the person I am today.

Every experience that I've had, as painful, as unfair, and challenging as they may have seemed, needed to occur to make me strong, forgiving, perseverant, and gave me tenacity and my soul.

I am here.

I am here.

Home and complete.

I am still standing.

I choose to see each obstacle as an opportunity to grow.

I release all negative energy that hurts me.

I am a powerful being of possibility and today I am stepping into that greatness.

I am allowing my light to shine.

No longer will I dim the light.

Today forward it will shine.

Today I stand in my greatness.

I recognize my genius.

I embrace my brilliance.

I love myself.

The world has a need for me.

I have a purpose.

I am unique.

Breathe in and breathe out.

I can and I will do things to promote healing in my life.

I can handle this one step at a time.

I love myself.

I will let my light shine.

My problem has a solution.

I will work on a plan.

I will ask the universe for divine guidance.

I am a survivor.

I am willing to listen to what my body is telling me.

I refuse to give up because I haven't tried all the possible ways.

I will inhale confidence and exhale doubt.

I may be one in 7 billion, but I'm also ONE in 7 billion.

I am smart.

I believe I can change the world.

I am important.

Today, I will celebrate me.

I matter.

No longer will I dim my light so that others won't feel insecure in my presence.

No longer will I dim my light to make sure I am acceptable.

No longer will I dim my light for fear of other people's perceptions of me.

So today in this moment, in this meditation, I declare my greatness.

I no longer shrink to fit in the small crevices of the world.

I stand boldly and open doors.

I am a champion.

I am ready for such a time as this.

I just need to take a breath.

Breathe in my readiness.

Exhale my doubt.

Exhale my worry my fears.

Breathe in my acceptance.

Breathe out my doubt.

I now acknowledge out loud that I am ready.

I now acknowledge out loud that I've been ready for a very long time.

I have a purpose that I am fulfilling.

Breathe in and breathe out.

Take another deep breath with a sigh.

Rub your hands together and generate a little heat between them.

Once they're warm, put them on your eyes.

Take these last precious moments to acknowledge your

commitment to this practice to bringing the light and the magic with you into your daily life.
When you're ready, put your hands down and gently open your eyes.
Namaste

Key Takeaway:

Meditation and developing a daily practice can be an important part of your treatment plan, as well as a valuable tool for your family/friends. There are a variety of ways to meditate. Find the one(s) that work best for you to help lessen your stress, bring more calmness into your life, and create daily moments of peacefulness.

GETTING HELP

HELPFUL RESOURCES

The final chapter of *The Ultimate Guide for Bipolar Disorder* is dedicated to providing you with a detailed list of valuable resources. Below you will find links to websites focused on educating and treating bipolar disorder, identifying recovery centers and support groups, and impactful mental health organizations. Additionally, links to information about various mental health issues and addictions are provided, as well as useful apps and books.

For those listening to the audiobook, please download the attached PDF which lists these resources and their links. Only the organizations' name will be read and not the full URL.

U.S. SUICIDE HOTLINES AND IMMEDIATE TELEPHONE SUPPORT

If you or someone you know needs immediate help in the U.S., call any of the lines below to talk to someone in your local area. They can listen to you and direct you to local resources if further assistance is needed. If someone has talked to you about suicide, and you believe they are currently a threat to themselves or someone else, but won't take your help, call 911.

- **National Suicide Prevention Lifeline**

Dial 988

(800) 273-8255 or 1-800-273-TALK

- **National Suicide Prevention Lifeline: Spanish Language Available**

(888) 628-9454

- **National Suicide Prevention Lifeline: Deaf & Hard of Hearing Options**

(800) 799-4889

- **National Suicide Prevention Hotline**

(800) 784-2433 or 1-800-SUICIDE

- **National Suicide Prevention Hotline: Spanish Speaking**

(800) 784-2432 or 1-800-SUICIDA

- **National Alliance on Mental Illness**
(Information, Resources, Support)

800-950-NAMI (6264)

(Monday-Friday, 10 a.m. – 10 p.m. ET)

Text: 62640

Webchat: www.nami.org/help

Email: helpline@nami.org

- **Teen to Teen Peer Counseling Hotline**

(877) 968-8454 or 1-877-YOUTHLINE

- **TrevorLifeLine for LGBTQ Support**

(866) 488-7386

- **Trans Lifeline**

(877) 565-8860

You can also text HOME to 741741 to connect with a crisis counselor from crisistextline.org.

FINDING PROVIDERS (DOCTORS, PSYCHIATRISTS, THERAPISTS) WHO SPECIALIZE IN BIPOLAR DISORDER

- **Depression and Bipolar Support Alliance – Healthcare Providers**

www.dbsalliance.org/wellness/treatment-options/finding-a-health-care-provider

- **Health Grades – Bipolar Disorder Specialists**

www.healthgrades.com/right-care/bipolar-disorder/find-a-specialist-who-treats-bipolar-disorder

- **Thriveworks – Therapists and Psychiatrists**

www.thriveworks.com

- **Betterhelp - Online Therapy**

www.Betterhelp.com

- **Healthline – Finding the right Therapist**

www.healthline.com/health/bipolar-disorder/finding-the-right-therapist

BIPOLAR DISORDER MEDICATIONS

- **Help Guide – Bipolar Disorder Medications**

www.helpguide.org/articles/bipolar-disorder/bipolar-medication-guide.htm

- **Medical News Today – Medications for Bipolar Disorder**

www.medicalnewstoday.com/articles/324388

SUPPLEMENTS AND ALTERNATIVE TREATMENTS

- **Healthline – Alternative Treatments**

www.healthline.com/health/bipolar-disorder/alternative-treatments

- **TRE® Trauma Releasing Exercises**

www.traumaprevention.com

SUPPORT GROUPS

- **Depression and Bipolar Support Alliance – Support Groups**

www.dbsalliance.org/support/chapters-and-support-groups/find-a-support-group

- **Healthline – Bipolar Disorder Support Groups**

www.healthline.com/health/mental-health/bipolar-support-groups

- **National Alliance on Mental Illness – Family Support Groups**

www.nami.org/Support-Education/Support-Groups/NAMI-Family-Support-Group

- **Psych Central - Bipolar Disorder Support Groups**

www.psychcentral.com/reviews/best-online-bipolar-disorder-support-groups

- **Support Group Central**

www.supportgroupscentral.com/index.cfm

- **International Foundation for Research and Education on Depression–Specialized Support Group Resources**

www.ifred.org/individual-support

TWELVE-STEP AND COMMUNITY-BASED PROGRAMS

- **Adult Children of Alcoholics**

www.adultchildren.org

- **Alcoholics Anonymous**

www.aa.org

- **Codependents Anonymous**

www.coda.org

- **Dual Diagnosis Anonymous**

www.ddainc.org/online-dda-meetings

- **Marijuana Anonymous**

www.marijuana-anonymous.org

- **Methamphetamine Anonymous**

www.crystalmeth.org

- **Narcotics Anonymous**

www.na.org

- **Refuge Recovery–A Buddhist-Oriented, Non-Theistic Recovery Program**

www.refugerecovery.org

- **Smart Recovery–Life Beyond Addiction**

www.smartrecovery.org

TREATMENT CENTERS

- **Bipolar Lives**

www.bipolar-lives.com/bipolar-treatment-centers.html

- **American Residential Treatment Association**

www.artausa.org/residential-mental-health-directory

- **Substance Abuse and Mental Health Services Administration**

www.samhsa.gov/find-treatment

- **Luxury Rehabs**

www.luxuryrehabs.com/condition/bipolar

ADDITIONAL IMPORTANT RESOURCES

Websites & PDFs

- **Suicide and Crisis Lifeline**

www.988lifeline.org

- **NeuRa–Research on Bipolar Disorder**

www.neura.edu.au/health/bipolar-disorder

- **NeuRa–Bipolar Disorders Library**

www.library.neura.edu.au/category/bipolar-disorder

- **National Institute of Mental Health–Digital Shareables on Bipolar Disorder**

www.nimh.nih.gov/get-involved/digital-shareables/shareable-resources-on-bipolar-disorder

- **National Alliance on Mental Illness – Helpline Resources Directory (PDF)**

www.nami.org/NAMI/media/NAMI-Media/Images/FactSheets/HelpLine-Resource-Directory.pdf

- **BPHope – Hope and Harmony for People with Bipolar**

www.bphope.com

- **WebMD–Bipolar Disorder Resources**

www.webmd.com/bipolar-disorder/guide/bipolar-disorder-resources-1

- **Centre for Clinical Interventions–Downloadable Information Sheets**

www.cci.health.wa.gov.au/Resources/Looking-After-Yourself/Bipolar

- **International Bipolar Foundation**

www.ibpf.org

- **Everyday Health – Bipolar Disorder Resources**

www.everydayhealth.com/bipolar-disorder/guide/resources

- **American Academy of Child and Adolescent Psychiatry – Bipolar Disorder Resource Center**

www.aacap.org/aacap/Families_and_Youth/Resource_Centers/Bipolar_Disorder_Resource_Center/Home.aspx

- **Juvenile Bipolar Research Foundation**

www.jbrf.org

- **National Institute of Mental Health – Help for Mental Illnesses**

www.nimh.nih.gov/health/find-help

- **Hopeful Minds–Hope Is Teachable**

www.hopefulminds.org

- **International Foundation for Research and Education on Depression (iFred)**

www.ifred.org

- **Merilu Hill–Guided Meditations**

www.meriluhill.com/freebies

Apps for Tracking and Planning

- **Bipolar Mood Tracker**

https://apps.apple.com/us/app/emoods-bipolar-mood-tracker/id1184456130

- **iMoodJournal**

www.imoodjournal.com

- **eMoods**

www.emoodtracker.com

- **MindDoc**

www.minddoc.com

- **Moodnotes**

www.thriveport.com/products/moodnotes

- **Daylio**

www.daylio.net

- **Depression and Bipolar Support Alliance: Wellness Tracker**

www.dbsalliance.org/wellness/wellness-toolbox/wellness-tracker

- **TherapistAid Habit Plan Worksheet**

www.therapistaid.com/therapy-worksheet/habit-plan#

Books and Audiobooks

Guided Meditations for Anxiety, Trauma, Addiction, and Self-Healing by The Mindfulness Mentors (Audiobook):

https://amzn.to/3YwZmfF

Girl, Be Fearless: It's Time to Make Your Dreams a Reality by Merilu Hill (Book and Audiobook):

https://amzn.to/3xsg3g4

CONCLUSION

— MICHELLE OBAMA

You have officially made it to the end of *The Ultimate Guide for Bipolar Disorder*, though your journey with bipolar disorder will continue long after you close this book. Throughout these eight chapters, you have taken in an incredible amount of information. From the basics of bipolar disorder to effective ways to manage your symptoms, you have been given a foundation on which you can continue to build your knowledge of this complex mental illness.

This guide began with an introduction to a dear friend of mine. Don's personal experience with bipolar disorder has been a combination of struggles and victories. Through his vulnerability and willingness to share his story with others, you were able to understand how bipolar disorder can dictate every aspect of a person's life, including their relationships, financial stability, and sense of self. As you read about Don's experience, you learned the intimate details of a man struggling to cope with his diagnosis. In the end, however, you saw that success in the face of bipolar disorder is possible when you live with determination and hope.

In chapter two, you were given a full explanation of bipolar disorder symptoms, behaviors, and misconceptions. Alongside an in-depth description of the types of bipolar disorder, you were made aware of the harmful stereotypes that are used against people with the condition. For each myth and misunderstanding, there is a fact that can change society's perception. The second chapter also explained the various causes of bipolar disorder, in addition to the discoveries that have been made over decades of scientific research. From here, with a new understanding of the disorder, you hopefully found yourself starting to heal.

Chapter three focused on the importance of acknowledging when you or your loved one's symptoms have begun to show devastating impacts. You learned that, although it can be a long process, receiving treatment will help your bipolar disorder management more than anything else. This chapter taught you what can happen if your bipolar disorder is left untreated. Brain damage, emotional instability, and dangerous behaviors are just a few of the consequences of avoiding treatment. You read about the diagnostic process and the different healthcare professionals you may encounter when receiving treatment. You were encouraged to ask questions, seek referrals, and be patient while finding providers that fit your needs. The third chapter even taught you the many different treatment and support options that exist today. Medications and therapy are scientifically-proven ways to treat bipolar disorder effectively, but there are plenty of other methods for managing your symptoms. Activities like meditation, routine-building, and alternative medicines have been shown to help those affected by the disorder.

In chapter four, this book emphasized the importance of building a good support system. Family, friends, doctors, and colleagues can play significant roles in your treatment. You were taught about authentic communication and how to overcome the discomfort that comes with speaking about mental illness. You learned how to set healthy boundaries and what to do when those boundaries are not honored. Most importantly, you were shown how to educate your loved ones about your personal experience with bipolar disorder. After this influx of valuable information, you were provided hope by reading about the successes of people with bipolar disorder. Just like with my friend Don, these stories cast a bright light on the positive outcomes of treatment and recovery.

These stories of hope segue wayed easily into chapter five, where we discussed The Five Keys for Hope™. This method of encouraging positivity was developed by another friend of mine, whose professional and personal experience with mental illness has inspired many. These Five Keys taught you how to manage stress, create happy habits, take inspired action, find your community, and eliminate challenges in your life. Learning these skills and practicing them daily can take you from feeling hopeless about your bipolar disorder to feeling hopeful about your future.

In chapter six, techniques for building and maintaining healthy routines were provided. You became aware of the countless benefits that creating a routine can have on your bipolar disorder management. Routines are incredibly useful when you are struggling to control mental and emotional struggles. This chapter encouraged you to build a schedule you can follow with ease while promoting a healthy lifestyle. Your overall well-being depends on your life's stability, which is why creating routines can be so beneficial. With the chaos that comes from bipolar disorder, having as much stability as possible is essential.

When it comes to managing a routine, replacing bad habits with healthy ones can make a significant difference. Chapter six taught you what it means to replace a habit that no longer serves you. You also learned how to plan new habits, step by step. With this knowledge, you have the ability to completely change your life for the better, including your experience with bipolar disorder.

The following chapter described the benefits of adding daily meditations to your routine. Meditation is a practice that has been used to help people for millennia. The act of clearing your mind to become calm and balanced is not only a great way to counteract symptoms of bipolar disorder, but a fantastic method for gaining clarity in general. When you meditate, even for a short period of time, you allow yourself to focus your attention on the calm inside of you, instead of on the many stressors life throws your way.

Chapter seven provided you with multiple meditations and affirmations to encourage positivity in your life. These practices have been proven to help with addiction recovery, anxiety, trauma healing, and other emotional struggles. It was my absolute pleasure to bring these specific meditations into your life. I hope they continue to help you and your loved ones heal throughout your journeys.

Finally, you reached the chapter in this book that I hope will be one that you will refer to time and time again. In chapter eight, you were given the space to explore the many resources that exist to guide you in your understanding of mental illness, and bipolar disorder specifically. My ultimate goal for this book is for it to be a source of valuable information for you. With the resources provided in the final chapter, you have been given a map to continue your exploration of the complexities of mental well-being. You have been given the key to access supportive communities, treatment centers, and organizations dedicated to educating and destigmatizing mental illness. I urge you to make good use of this resource list now and in the future.

Now that you have come to the end of this guide, you have the ability to educate others on bipolar disorder.

You have learned the truth about the condition and can break the stigma that bipolar people are *crazy* or *unstable*. Your knowledge has enabled you to change how the world views bipolar disorder and other mental illnesses.

You have read the true success stories of many people diagnosed with bipolar disorder. You know that it is possible to live a happy, healthy life, regardless of your diagnosis. It is even possible to maintain meaningful relationships. Bipolar disorder may not be curable, but there are many treatments and strategies that can be used to manage one's symptoms effectively. With these methods, along with others described in this book, you can transition from a place of chaos to a safe, comfortable mindset. There is light at the end of the tunnel, you just have to have hope.

I would like to express my sincere gratitude and acknowledgment of the friends and colleagues that have helped me create this book:

- Kathryn Goetzke and her teams at iFred and HopefulMinds
- Dr. Tanya Chase, Psy.D. Psychology
- Paul Huff
- MJ and Helena
- Pauline Evanosky

- My AIA Mastermind group (you know who you are!)

Your willingness to be a part of this project is truly appreciated.

SHOW SOMEONE ELSE THE WAY FORWARD

Now that you've taken that first step, you can help other people find the same path to treatment and finding support for bipolar disorder.

Simply by leaving your honest opinion of this book on Amazon, you'll show new readers where they can find the information you've used to set you on your way.

Thank you for your support. We're all on a journey – and as you set forth on your own, you can help someone else out on theirs.

Scan the QR code for a quick review!

Want to be inspired each day? Follow me on
FaceBook at:

www.facebook.com/sunflowerhousepublishing

Or scan the QR code below!

REFERENCES

33 of the best meditation quotes. (2021). Headspace. https://www.headspace.com/meditation/quotes

Addiction Centers. (2022, September 15). *Benzodiazepine Addiction: Symptoms and signs.* American Addiction Centers. https://americanaddictioncenters.org/benzodiazepine/symptoms-and-signs

Adult Children of Alcoholics & Dysfunctional Families. (2018). *Welcome to adult children of alcoholics & dysfunctional families.* Adult Children. https://adultchildren.org/

Alcoholics Anonymous. (2023). *Alcoholics anonymous.* AA. https://www.aa.org/

Altrogge, S. (2022, December 20). *12 morning and evening routines that will set up each day for success.* Zapier. https://zapier.com/blog/daily-routines/

American Psychiatric Association. (2002). *Treating bipolar disorder: A quick reference guide.* https://bhdp.sccgov.org/sites/g/files/exjcpb716/files/Treating-Bipolar-Disorder.pdf

Best bipolar treatment centers of 2023 (with pricing). (n.d.). Luxury Rehabs. https://luxuryrehabs.com/condition/bipolar/

Bipolar disorder resource center. (2022, July). AACAP. https://www.aacap.org/AACAP/Families_and_Youth/Resource_Centers/Bipolar_Disorder_Resource_Center/Home.aspx

Bipolar disorder self-help resources - information sheets. (2019). Centre for Clinical Interventions. https://www.cci.health.wa.gov.au/Resources/Looking-After-Yourself/Bipolar

BPHope. https://www.bphope.com/

BP Magazine. (2017, August 7). *Top 6 mood-tracking apps for bipolar.* BP Hope. https://www.bphope.com/bipolar-buzz/bipolar-lifestyle-top-6-apps-to-track-your-moods/

Brainy Quote. (2023). *Michelle Obama quotes.* BrainyQuote. https://

www.brainyquote.com/quotes/michelle_obama_415504?src=
t_hope

Brenner, B. (2019, September 16). *Creativity is your secret advantage for
mental health and well-being.* Therapy Group of NYC. https://
nyctherapy.com/therapists-nyc-blog/creativity-is-your-secret-
advantage-for-mental-health-and-well-being/

Cha, B., Kim, J. H., Ha, T. H., Chang, J. S., & Ha, K. (2009). *Polarity of the
first episode and time to diagnosis of bipolar I disorder.* Psychiatry
Investigation, 6(2), 96. https://doi.org/10.4306/pi.2009.6.2.96

CoDA. (n.d.). *A program of recovery from codependence.* Co-Dependents
Anonymous. https://coda.org/

Compare adult residential psychiatric treatment centers in the USA. (2023).
ARTA USA. https://artausa.org/residential-mental-health-
directory/

Creativity. (2019, January 31). GoodTherapy. https://www.goodther
apy.org/blog/psychpedia/creativity

Crystal Meth Anonymous. (2023). *Crystal meth anonymous – crystal meth
recovery.* Crystal Meth Anonymous. https://www.crystalmeth.org/

Davidson, K. (2020, February 5). *Mood food: 9 foods that can really boost
your spirits.* Healthline Media. https://www.healthline.com/nutri
tion/mood-food

DDA, Inc. (2023). *Online DDA meetings.* Dual Diagnosis Anonymous.
https://ddainc.org/online-dda-meetings/

Digital shareables on bipolar disorder. (n.d.). National Institute of Mental
Health. https://www.nimh.nih.gov/get-involved/digital-share
ables/shareable-resources-on-bipolar-disorder

Dome, P., Rihmer, Z., & Gonda, X. (2019). *Suicide risk in bipolar disorder:
A brief review.* Medicina, 55(8), 403. https://doi.org/10.3390/
medicina55080403

Dunleavy, B. P. (2019, October 21). *Bipolar disorder resources.* Everyday
Health. https://www.everydayhealth.com/bipolar-disorder/guide/
resources/

Elliot, S. (2013, May 13). *Find treatment.* SAMHSA. https://www.
samhsa.gov/find-treatment

Epstein, L. J. (2008, December 15). *Sleep and mood.* Harvard Medical

School. https://healthysleep.med.harvard.edu/need-sleep/whats-in-it-for-you/mood

Find a local support group. (n.d.). Depression and Bipolar Support Alliance. https://www.dbsalliance.org/support/chapters-and-support-groups/find-a-support-group/

Find a Specialist Who Treats Bipolar Disorder. (2023). HealthGrades. https://www.healthgrades.com/right-care/bipolar-disorder/find-a-specialist-who-treats-bipolar-disorder

Finding a health care provider. (n.d.). Depression and Bipolar Support Alliance. https://www.dbsalliance.org/wellness/treatment-options/finding-a-health-care-provider/

Flanigan, R. L. (2022, October 11). *Assembling your bipolar care team.* BP Hope. https://www.bphope.com/assembling-your-bipolar-care-team/

Freebies. (n.d.). Merilu Hill. https://meriluhill.com/freebies

Gavin, K. (2017, December 15). *After searching 12 years for bipolar disorder's cause, a team concludes it has many.* Lab Blog; Michigan Medicine. https://labblog.uofmhealth.org/body-work/after-searching-12-years-for-bipolar-disorders-cause-a-team-concludes-it-has-many

Gluck, S. (2020). *Quotes on bipolar disorder.* Healthy Place. https://www.healthyplace.com/insight/quotes/quotes-on-bipolar

Goss, R. (2019, October 15). *How to deal with someone who doesn't respect personal boundaries.* INLP Center. https://inlpcenter.org/how-to-deal-with-someone-who-doesnt-respect-personal-boundaries/

Group profile: Depression and bipolar support alliance. (2022). Support Groups Central. https://www.supportgroupscentral.com/groups_detail.cfm?cid=18

Gutknecht, L. (n.d.). *Boost your self-esteem with 7 simple daily routines.* Foodspring Magazine. https://www.foodspring.co.uk/magazine/self-esteem#:~:text=To%20help%20build%20self%2Desteem

Harvard Health Publishing. (2022, February 2). *Six relaxation techniques to reduce stress.* Harvard Health. https://www.health.harvard.edu/mind-and-mood/six-relaxation-techniques-to-reduce-stress

Healthline. (2019, November 6). *10 alternative treatments for bipolar disorder*. Healthline Media. https://www.healthline.com/health/bipolar-disorder/alternative-treatments

Hiers, T. (2021, June 30). *How to find and choose a good psychiatrist.* Thriveworks. https://thriveworks.com/blog/how-to-find-and-choose-a-good-psychiatrist/

Hill, M. (2022). *Girl, be fearless: It's time to make your dreams a reality.* Merilu Hill.

Hirschfeld, R. M. A. (2007). Screening for bipolar disorder. *Bipolar Disorder: Closing the Effective Care Gap, 13*(7). AJMC. https://www.ajmc.com/view/nov07-2656ps164-s169

Home. (n.d.). IFred. https://www.ifred.org/

Hooks, B. (2018). *All about love: New visions.* Harper Perennial.

Hopeful minds. (2014). *Hopeful Minds.* https://hopefulminds.org/

Huizen, J. (2023, January 9). *Medications for bipolar disorder: List, types, and side effects.* Medical News Today. https://www.medicalnewstoday.com/articles/324388

IFS Institute. (2023). *What is Internal Family Systems?* IFS Institute. https://ifs-institute.com/

Improvement Pill. (2017). 3 habits that will change your life [YouTube Video]. In *YouTube.* https://www.youtube.com/watch?v=7DSscQlSZR4

Improvement Pill. (2021). How to fix any habit - (the habit troubleshooter) [Youtube Video]. In *Youtube.* https://www.youtube.com/watch?v=hTQy-PW7xkU

International Bipolar Foundation. *(n.d.). Please stop saying "bipolar" when you mean unpredictable or broken.* International Bipolar Foundation. https://ibpf.org/articles/please-stop-saying-bipolar-when-you-mean-unpredictable-or-broken/

International bipolar foundation. (n.d.). International Bipolar Foundation. https://ibpf.org/

Jaffe, D. J. (n.d.). *Bipolar disorder: Symptoms, treatments, recovery rates.* Mental Illness Policy Org. https://mentalillnesspolicy.org/medical/bipolar-facts.html

Jenner, E. (2020). Woman having a video call [Online Image]. In *Pexels.* https://www.pexels.com/photo/woman-having-a-video-call-

4031818/

Juergens, J. (2022, December 16). *Bipolar disorder and addiction.* Addiction Center. https://www.addictioncenter.com/addiction/bipolar-disorder/

Juvenile Bipolar Research Foundation. https://www.jbrf.org/

Kerslake, R. (2022, April 26). *8 best bipolar support groups of 2021.* Healthline; Healthline Media. https://www.healthline.com/health/mental-health/bipolar-support-groups

Kleinhandler, D. (2017, August 18). *The secret of your future is hidden in your daily routine.* LinkedIn Corporation. https://www.linkedin.com/pulse/secret-your-future-hidden-daily-routine-mike-murdock-kleinhandler/

Krause, S. (2016, January 27). *5 interesting facts about habits.* Medium. https://medium.com/@susannekrausedx/5-interesting-facts-about-habits-76fffa6f291f

Larkin, E. (2020, October 25). *How to create a daily routine that works for you.* The Spruce. https://www.thespruce.com/how-to-create-a-daily-routine-2648007

Luxenbug, M. (2016, August 2). *30 things not to say to those with bipolar disorder.* International Bipolar Foundation. https://ibpf.org/30-things-not-to-say-to-those-with-bipolar-disorder/

Marijuana Anonymous. (2023). *Marijuana anonymous world services.* Marijuana Anonymous World Services. https://marijuana-anonymous.org/

Mayo Clinic. (2021a, February 16). *Bipolar disorder.* Mayo Clinic. https://www.mayoclinic.org/diseases-conditions/bipolar-disorder/symptoms-causes/syc-20355955

Mayo Clinic. (2021b, February 16). *Bipolar disorder - diagnosis and treatment.* Mayo Clinic. https://www.mayoclinic.org/diseases-conditions/bipolar-disorder/diagnosis-treatment/drc-20355961

Meditation statistics: How & why people meditate in 2020. (2020, January 2). Mellowed. https://mellowed.com/meditation-statistics/

Mental Health Foundation. (n.d.). *Nature: How connecting with nature benefits our mental health.* Mental Health Foundation. https://www.mentalhealth.org.uk/our-work/research/nature-how-connecting-nature-benefits-our-mental-health

Miasnikov, C. (2021). *Myths and facts of bipolar disorder.* NAMI. https://www.nami.org/Blogs/NAMI-Blog/May-2021/Myths-and-Facts-of-Bipolar-Disorder

Miklowitz, D. (2019, April 12). *Different types of therapy for bipolar disorder.* NAMI. https://www.nami.org/Blogs/NAMI-Blog/April-2019/Different-Types-of-Therapy-for-Bipolar-Disorder

Miller, G., & Pedersen, T. (2022, March 15). *The 7 best online bipolar disorder support groups in 2022.* Psych Central. https://psychcentral.com/reviews/best-online-bipolar-disorder-support-groups

Mojica Rey, C. (2003, May 6). *Study suggests bipolar disorder may cause progressive brain damage.* UCSF. https://www.ucsf.edu/news/2003/05/97207/study-suggests-bipolar-disorder-may-cause-progressive-brain-damage

Moore, M. (2021, September 13). *Not for everyone: 8 red flags you're with the wrong therapist.* Psych Central. https://psychcentral.com/lib/red-flags-a-clinician-isnt-right-for-you

NAMI. (2020). *Bipolar disorder.* National Alliance on Mental Illness. https://www.nami.org/About-Mental-Illness/Mental-Health-Conditions/Bipolar-Disorder/Overview

NAMI family support group. (2023). NAMI. https://www.nami.org/Support-Education/Support-Groups/NAMI-Family-Support-Group

NAMI *Helpline Resources Directory (PDF). (2023).* www.nami.org/NAMI/media/NAMI-Media/Images/FactSheets/HelpLine-Resource-Directory.pdf

Narcotics Anonymous World Services. (2023). *NA.* Narcotics Anonymous World Services. https://na.org/

National Institute of Mental Health. (2019, August). *Help for mental illnesses.* NIMH. https://www.nimh.nih.gov/health/find-help

National Institute of Mental Health. (2020, January). *Bipolar disorder.* National Institute of Mental Health. https://www.nimh.nih.gov/health/topics/bipolar-disorder

NeuRA Library. (n.d.). *Adjunctive and alternative treatments.* NeuRA. https://library.neura.edu.au/category/bipolar-disorder/treat

ments-bipolar-disorder/physical-treatments-bipolar-disorder/phar maceutical-physical-treatments-bipolar-disorder/adjunctive-and-alternative-treatments/

NHS. (2021a, February 11). *Diagnosis - bipolar disorder.* NHS. https://www.nhs.uk/mental-health/conditions/bipolar-disorder/diagnosis/

NHS. (2021b, February 11). *Treatment - bipolar disorder.* NHS. https://www.nhs.uk/mental-health/conditions/bipolar-disorder/treatment/

NHS. (2023, January 3). *Causes - bipolar disorder.* NHS. https://www.nhs.uk/mental-health/conditions/bipolar-disorder/causes/#:~

NYU Langone Health. (n.d.). *Diagnosing bipolar disorder.* NYU Langone. https://nyulangone.org/conditions/bipolar-disorder/diagnosis

Olsson, R. (2020, June 22). *Common myths about bipolar disorder.* Banner Health. https://www.bannerhealth.com/healthcareblog/better-me/myths-about-bipolar-disorder

Pagán, C. N. (2016, November 21). *What should I do if my bipolar meds don't work?* WebMD. https://www.webmd.com/bipolar-disorder/features/bipolar-meds-not-working

Palisoc, J. (2018, March 29). *Why people with bipolar disorder can feel hopeful about the future.* Your Health Matters. https://health.sunny brook.ca/mental-health/bipolar-disorder-hopeful-future/

Payne, J. (n.d.). *Bipolar relationships: What to expect.* Johns Hopkins Medicine. https://www.hopkinsmedicine.org/health/conditions-and-diseases/mood-disorders/bipolar-relationships-what-to-expect

Rabon, M. (2022, June 7). *5 ways acknowledging your mental health leads to action.* IBelieve. https://www.ibelieve.com/health-beauty/5-ways-acknowledging-your-mental-health-leads-to-action.html

Reiff Ellis, R. (2020, September 2). *Long-Term effects of bipolar disorder.* WebMD. https://www.webmd.com/bipolar-disorder/long-term-effects-of-bipolar-disorder

Refuge Recovery. (n.d.). *Refuge recovery world services.* Refuge Recovery World Services. https://www.refugerecovery.org/

Robinson, M. (2017, June). *Please stop believing these 8 harmful bipolar disorder myths.* Healthline Media. https://www.healthline.com/health/8-harmful-bipolar-disorder-myths-you-need-to-stop-believing

RTOR. (2020, July 1). *Top 7 signs to look for in bipolar disorder.* RTOR. https://www.rtor.org/2020/07/01/top-7-signs-to-look-for-in-bipolar-disorder/

Salters-Pedneault, K. (2020, December 6). *How a structured schedule helps borderline personality disorder.* Verywell Mind. https://www.verywellmind.com/how-to-plan-structured-activities-425408

Schwartz, R. (2023). *Evolution of the Internal Family Systems model.* IFS Institute. https://ifs-institute.com/resources/articles/evolution-internal-family-systems-model-dr-richard-schwartz-ph-d

Sensory calming activities. (n.d.). Sensory Processing Disorder Parent Support. https://sensoryprocessingdisorderparentsupport.com/sensory-calming-activities.php

Skyland Trail. (2017, August 25). *A positive outlook on living with bipolar disorder.* Skyland Trail. https://www.skylandtrail.org/a-positive-outlook-on-living-with-bipolar-disorder

SMART Recovery. (2022). *Ready to overcome your addiction?* SMART Recovery. https://www.smartrecovery.org/

Smith, M., Robinson, L., & Segal, J. (2022, December 15). *Bipolar disorder medication guide.* HelpGuide. https://www.helpguide.org/articles/bipolar-disorder/bipolar-medication-guide.htm

Sorensen, D. (2022, April 20). *How to ask for help.* Psyche. https://psyche.co/guides/how-to-ask-for-help-without-discomfort-or-apology

Stanborough, R. J. (2020, December 15). *Dehydration and anxiety: Understanding the connection.* Healthline Media. https://www.healthline.com/health/anxiety/dehydration-and-anxiety

Stephens, S. (2020, September 25). *Behavioral change: Step-By-Step bipolar success stories.* BP Hope. https://www.bphope.com/step-by-step-bipolar-success-stories/

Tartakovsky, M. (2014, February 26). *How to know your boundaries: 4 steps.* Psych Central. https://psychcentral.com/blog/how-to-figure-out-your-boundaries#1

Tartakovsky, M. (2022, March 17). *How to find the right therapist for bipolar disorder*. Healthline Media. https://www.healthline.com/health/bipolar-disorder/finding-the-right-therapist

Team Bipolar Lives. (2019, October 9). *Bipolar treatment centers*. Bipolar Lives. https://www.bipolar-lives.com/bipolar-treatment-centers.html

The 988 Suicide and Crisis Lifeline. (n.d.). *Home*. 988 Lifeline. https://988lifeline.org/?utm_source=google&utm_medium=web&utm_campaign=onebox

The Mindfulness Mentors. (2022). *Guided meditations for anxiety, trauma, addiction, and self-healing: 2+ hours of guided meditations to help you overcome your anxiety and past trauma to live with a clear mind and find inner peace*. Ethos Creative Media Agency. https://www.amazon.com/Guided-Meditations-Anxiety-Addiction-Self-Healing/dp/B09WNH3523/ref=sr_1_1?crid=3VK0XSM-MV46PV&keywords=guided+meditations+for+anxiety%2C+trauma%2C+addiction%2C+and+self-healing&qid=1670349910&s=books&sprefix=guided+meditations+for+anxiety%2C+trauma%2C+addiction%2C+and+self-healing%2Cstripbooks%2C83&sr=1-1

The Recovery Village. (2022, July 20). *Effects of alcohol on bipolar disorder and medications*. The Recovery Village Drug and Alcohol Rehab. https://www.therecoveryvillage.com/alcohol-abuse/alcoholism-bipolar-disorder

Therapist Aid. (2020). *Habit plan*. In Therapist Aid. Therapist Aid LLC. https://www.therapistaid.com/worksheets/habit-plan

Trauma Prevention. (n.d.). *Tension and trauma releasing exercises*. TRE for ALL. https://traumaprevention.com/

True Citrus. (2018, July 27). *A simple way to create new habits: Use the three*. True Citrus. https://www.truelemon.com/blogs/tc/simple-way-create-new-habits

Tzeses, J. (2021, December 16). *How to set up your bipolar support squad*. Health Central. https://www.healthcentral.com/article/your-bipolar-support-system

Vandergriendt, C. (2020, September 30). *17 signs of a good therapist.*

Healthline; Healthline Media. https://www.healthline.com/health/signs-of-a-good-therapist

Villines, Z. (2020, March 26). *Psychiatry 101: How to become a psychiatrist.* GoodTherapy. https://www.goodtherapy.org/for-professionals/personal-development/become-a-therapist/article/psychiatry-101-how-to-become-psychiatrist

Ward, C. (2021, March 5). *Bipolar Disorder Test.* Psych Central. https://psychcentral.com/quizzes/bipolar-quiz

Wasmer Andrews, L. (2017, November 14). *10 warning signs of bipolar disorder.* Everyday Health. https://www.everydayhealth.com/emotional-health/bipolar-disorder/10-warning-signs-bipolar-disorder/

WebMD. (2003, February 7). *Bipolar disorder.* WebMD. https://www.webmd.com/bipolar-disorder/mental-health-bipolar-disorder

WebMD. (2021, October 7). *Bipolar disorder resources.* WebMD. https://www.webmd.com/bipolar-disorder/guide/bipolar-disorder-resources-1

WebMD. (2022a, March 17). *Talking to friends and family about your bipolar disorder.* WebMD. https://www.webmd.com/bipolar-disorder/guide/talking-to-friends-family#:~

WebMD. (2022b, October 31). *Bipolar disorder treatment.* WebMD. https://www.webmd.com/bipolar-disorder/guide/understanding-bipolar-disorder-treatment

Wellness tracker. (n.d.). Depression and Bipolar Support Alliance. https://www.dbsalliance.org/wellness/wellness-toolbox/wellness-tracker/

Wells, D. (2019, December 6). *How exercise can help bipolar disorder.* Healthline; Healthline Media. https://www.healthline.com/health/bipolar-disorder/exercise#outlook

World Population Review. (2020). *US states - ranked by population 2020.* World Population Review. https://worldpopulationreview.com/states

Yuko, E. (2022, September 13). *This is what it looks like to set personal and emotional boundaries.* Real Simple. https://www.realsimple.com/health/mind-mood/emotional-health/how-to-set-boundaries

Zencare. (2019, February 6). *Square breathing: How to reduce stress through breathwork*. The Couch: A Therapy & Mental Wellness Blog. https://blog.zencare.co/square-breathing/

IMAGE REFERENCES

Cowley, N. (2018). Man in blue and brown plaid dress shirt touching his hair [Online Image]. In *Pexels*. https://www.pexels.com/photo/man-in-blue-and-brown-plaid-dress-shirt-touching-his-hair-897817/

Holmes, K. (2020). Ethnic girl having video chat with teacher online on laptop [Online Image]. In *Pexels*. https://www.pexels.com/photo/ethnic-girl-having-video-chat-with-teacher-online-on-laptop-5905709/

Jess Bailey Designs. (2018). Person holding white stylus [Online Image]. In *Pexels*. https://www.pexels.com/photo/person-holding-white-stylus-768472/

Justesen, D. (2018). Temple square in spring [Online Image]. In *Unsplash*. https://unsplash.com/photos/3LJtSgD8KLs

Monstera. (2021). Crop anonymous black woman writing in notebook [Online Image]. In *Pexels*. https://www.pexels.com/photo/crop-anonymous-black-woman-writing-in-notebook-9430880/

Olsen, B. (2021). Thoughtful black man [Online Image]. In *Pexels*. https://www.pexels.com/photo/thoughtful-black-man-in-activewear-meditating-in-autumn-park-7869594/

Piacquadio, A. (2020). Collage of portraits of cheerful woman [Online Image]. In *Pexels*. https://www.pexels.com/photo/collage-of-portraits-of-cheerful-woman-3807758/

SHVETS Production. (2021). Crop psychologist writing on clipboard during psychotherapy session [Online Image]. In *Pexels*. https://www.pexels.com/photo/crop-psychologist-writing-on-clipboard-during-psychotherapy-session-7176036/

Tankilevitch, P. (2021). Women doing yoga [Online Image]. In *Pexels*.

https://www.pexels.com/photo/a-women-doing-yoga-together-8538987/

Thethe, B. (2019). Woman wearing a blue hat close-up photography [Online Image]. In *Pexels*. https://www.pexels.com/photo/women-wearing-a-blue-hat-close-up-photography-1958747/